"While it isn't necessary to know the language of a foreign country when you live abroad, studying that language can infinitely ease and illuminate your entrée there. Deborah Fallows underscores this lesson again and again in this compelling account of her own trials and triumphs with studying Mandarin while residing in Shanghai and Beijing. A linguist by training, Fallows shows how even small advancements such as mastering a single word or phrase can unlock grammatical and cultural secrets.... Over the course of her three-year immersion, her ever-deepening insights immeasurably enrich her engagement with China—and ours as well."

Don George, *National Geographic Traveler*

"The joy of this book is its sense of humour and adventure: Deb decided to live outside the expatriate ghetto: learning the language, drinking the water, living the real Chinese life like a laobaixing (ordinary person).Whether it'slearning not to say "please," or understanding why Chinese hate the number "4" or ordering take-away at a Chinese Taco Bell, Deb jumps in head-first and makes us laugh at her often comical embrace of this culture. I can't think of a better book for someone who wants to understand the lovable, infuriating and hilarious country that is China."

David Ignatius, *Washington Post*

"Dreaming in Chinese is original, entertaining, gracefully written and provides important insights into life and culture in contemporary China. Deborah Fallows is a gifted linguist who helps her readers understand the complexities of the Chinese language. But she does much more. She is an astute observer and through simple yet compelling anecdotes she helps her readers experience everyday life. This is a terrific book for anyone who wants to improve their understanding of this extraordinary country. "

**Laura D. Tyson, Professor of Global Management,
University of California at Berkeley**

Dreaming in Chinese

Dreaming in Chinese

Lessons in life, love and Mandarin

DEBORAH FALLOWS

First published in 2010 by
Short Books
3A Exmouth House
Pine Street
EC1R 0JH

This paperback edition published by Short Books in 2012

10 9 8 7 6 5 4 3 2 1

A CIP catalogue record for this book is available from the
British Library.

ISBN 9781780720852
Cover design © Georgia Vaux

Printed in Great Britain by CPI Group (UK) Ltd, Croydon,
CR0 4YY

For Jim

CONTENTS

Introduction

I FIRST SAW China in the summer of 1986. My husband and I had packed up our then small children, left our home in Washington DC, and gone to live in Japan and Southeast Asia for four years. We jumped at a chance that came our way to visit China for several weeks, after living in Tokyo and before heading for Kuala Lumpur.

The China we visited then was still emerging from the Cultural Revolution. Most of the young people, dressed in their drab Mao suits or simple cheap clothes, were seeing Westerners for the first time. They would race to scoop up our blond children in their arms for pictures and to practise "Hello! Hello!" in English. The Chinese who greeted us were light and playful; we felt their high-spirited welcome, especially after the constraints of living in traditional, culture-bound Japan.

My recollections of that brief time are in snap-shots: I bought bottles of bright orange soda that lay cooling on slabs of ice in vendors' carts. We went to the Beijing zoo, which was dreary and untidy, to look for pandas. The skies in Beijing and Shanghai and Hangzhou were clear and blue. We guessed that the cheerless, Stalinist government resthouses where we stayed were probably bugged. On our domestic airliner flying to the south of China, we sat toward the front of the plane in big overstuffed armchairs and held our collective breath on take-off, peering through gaps in the floorboards to see the tarmac racing by below.

Almost 25 years later, my husband and I set off to return to China for three years, where he would be reporting and writing long stories for the literary and political magazine he works for, *The Atlantic*. I would be working on my research for the Pew Internet Project, looking at internet use in China. This excursion fit into the pattern of our life, alternating several years at home in Washington DC, with several years out exploring the world.

We knew before we headed to China again that our old memories would seem quaint and charming, and that we would be in for a different kind of adventure this time in a modern, booming China. We did what we could to prepare: went to movies, read books, looked online, studied maps, talked to people who had been there before us. We got a glimpse here and an insight there, but we knew it wasn't adding up to much of anything. In the end we took a leap of faith and boarded the plane for Shanghai.

I did one other thing to prepare: I studied Mandarin a few nights a week for a few terms at Georgetown University in DC, figuring that a jumpstart on the language could only help as we tried to set up some kind of normal life in China. I have been studying languages and linguistics for almost all my life, and at least the *process* of studying the language felt comfortable to me, even if the language did not.

Our entry to China was rough. The first month went by in a daze, but our first impressions and experiences remain perfectly vivid to me: I could not recognise or utter a single word of the Chinese I had been studying, and I even wondered if my teacher had been teaching us Cantonese instead of Mandarin.[1] My husband said, in an anxious sweat, "I will never learn enough about China to write anything."

The hot Shanghai wind blew at 40 knots for many days, like the famous Santa Anas in California. My husband was very, very sick for ten days from drinking the water. We wondered if we were being followed, or if our phones were tapped.

Slowly, of course, everything began to change. My teacher had indeed been teaching me Mandarin,

---

1 A language note: colloquially, the terms Mandarin and Chinese are often used interchangeably. Technically, Chinese is a broader term that covers the family of many different languages and dialects of China, including Mandarin and Cantonese. Mandarin is the official language of the People's Republic of China, and it is the language I studied. I usually use the terms colloquially in this book. See Chapter 10 for much more on the languages of China.

although without the heavy Shanghai accent I heard all around me and later sorted out. My husband went on to write many, many articles about China and had the journalistic time of his life. We became immune to every germ we ran into and were never really sick again in China. The weather changed, although we grew never to expect the skies to be clear or the air to be fresh. We know people were indeed watching us, but far from being a bother, they would invite us out to lunch to keep an eye on us and were friendly.

As for the language, the longer we were in China, the more engaged I became with Chinese. Part of that experience was true tribulation: I worked and studied hard but felt like I was only inching forward, my progress barely measurable. Eventually, finally, I marked a few milestones, cause for much self-congratulation that was generally noted only by me: the first day I ventured out without my dictionary and did OK; my first complete phone conversation in Chinese; the first time I followed the entire plot of a soap opera episode on TV; and my pièce de résistance, the day I chewed out a Shanghai taxi driver in Chinese for an egregious overcharge, and got a refund of 100 RMB (about twelve US dollars).

The language paid me back in ways I hadn't fully anticipated. It was my lifeline to our everyday survival in China. My language foibles, many of which I have recounted in this book, taught me as much as my rare and random successes. The language also unexpectedly became my way of making some sense of China, my telescope into the country. Foreigners I met and knew in China used their different passions to help them interpret China: artists used China's art world, as others used Chinese cooking, or traditional medicine, or business, or music, or any number of things they knew about. I used the language, or more precisely, the study of the language.

As I tried to learn to speak Mandarin, I also learned about how the language works – its words, its sounds, its grammar and its history. I often found a connection between some point of the language – a particular word or the use of a phrase, for example – and how that point could elucidate something very "Chinese" I would encounter in my everyday life in China. The language helped me understand what I saw on the streets or on our travels around the country – how people made their livings, their habits, their behaviour toward each other, how they dealt with adversity, and how they celebrated.

This book is the story of what I learned about the Chinese language, and what the language taught me about China.

Wǒ ài nǐ!   I love you!

Chapter 1

The grammar of romance

ONE SPRING DAY in Beijing, I was trudging home from the local market with bags of bright vegetables and fresh, soft tofu. Few people were out, and my eyes were on the ground to watch my step around the minor rubble and broken bits of pavement. It was not a pretty walk. Then I heard it, *sotto voce* but clearly distinguishable above the whine of nearby traffic: "Hello, I love you. Buy my jade. I love you!"

I looked up as a handsome young man, a Uighur, strolled briskly past me, his hands full of jade bracelets. The Uighurs are a beleaguered minority in China, Moslems who came from central Asia. They are darkly attractive, with deep eyes and unruly hair. It's easy for a foreigner in China to feel a quick bond with the Uighurs, however irrational and unwarranted, for their western looks.

I knew this man must have come from the farthest northwestern edge of China, the Xinjiang region. The street signs there grow long and cluttered with scripts in Russian, Arabic, Chinese and English. Xinjiang is an outpost, lying beyond the deserts and mountains of Gansu Province. In Gansu, farmers till the soil around the crumbled remains at the end of the Great Wall as though it were a nuisance rather than a relic. When my husband and I recently travelled to Urumqi, Xinjiang's capital city, people stared at us curiously, still unused to foreigners.

Uighurs often journey from Xinjiang, travelling a thousand miles or more to sell their home region's plump, chewy raisins or sweet almonds to the city-slickers in Shanghai and Beijing. Some will sell jade. I imagine them bartering for their jade by dark of night in the bustling Xinjiang markets where I saw piles of ruby- and lapis-coloured rugs and knives made with ox horn handles.

The first time I bought raisins from a Uighur's overflowing pushcart, while we were in Shanghai, I took them home to wash them, hoping that enough sudsy scrubbing would immunise my husband and me against the germs that had passed through a hundred hands between a Xinjiang arbour and our apartment kitchen. I rinsed the raisins again and again, but each new bowl of water turned brown. I laid them out on a towel to dry, just as I had seen the farmers lay out their fiery red peppers along rural roadsides. The raisins grew fat with water, but sat uneaten; dull, tasteless and messy. Finally, I threw them away. Then I bought a second batch, which we dared to eat straight from the Uighur's cart. They were delicious. I kept buying raisins and have never washed them since. By now, we have eaten a lot of dirty raisins, and they haven't made us sicker than anything else in China has.

I didn't end up buying jade from the Uighur who called out that morning, but I fell for his "I love you" in an instant. *Wǒ ài nǐ*, I thought. How often I heard those words in China. *Wǒ ài nǐ* is the staple of pop songs, movie titles and ring tones on young girls' mobile phones. Rock stars dance to *wǒ ài nǐ* music on China TV's ever-popular Las Vegas-like extravaganzas.

While the word *ài*, to love, can be tossed around lightly in China, I also caught hints of something more complicated. Why, for example, do so many of the Chinese-Western couples we know describe the same mutual incompatability in romance? The Westerners lament that the Chinese can never quite utter the words "I love you", and never, ever in their native *wǒ ài nǐ*; the Chinese scoff that Westerners say "I love you" cavalierly, sounding hollow and insincere.

And why did one of my Chinese friends, upon learning that I have two sons, ask me which one I love more, as if love were some kind of a zero-sum calculation? It was a question so alien that it sent me on a mission to find the true Chinese meaning of *ài*.

I spent a few days with a woman named Julia, who explained to me her version of love and marriage in China. Julia is like many Chinese women in their thirties whom I have met; she has a husband, a career, a new baby and a mother-in-law who babysits. "Sounds like a good deal to me," I told Julia, thinking how many women in America struggle to arrange what comes as part of the filial bargain in China. For now, China's first generation of only children, like Julia, are becoming parents of only children. The four grandparents, often retired and living nearby, care for and dote on their only, shared grandchild. Pick any park in China, and you'll see smiling grandpas pushing buggies.

Julia figured, rightly, that my husband and I had been married for a long time. She said that I must love my husband very much to be married so long. An odd comment, I thought. I wasn't sure if it was a compliment, or a statement of longing, or an opening for a question back. "Of course," I said, and added rather lamely, "I'm sure you must love your husband a lot, too."

"Yes," she said, "I love him for now."

For now? Was this all about cold convenience? Did her husband and all those grandparents suspect she might be here right now confiding in me, someone she barely knew? Or was there something else, some veil across the language between us?

I found some clues in a novel that I bought after watching a Chinese girl, my seatmate on an interminable long-haul flight from San Francisco to Beijing, reading it straight through. The book has an intriguing title: *A Concise Chinese-English Dictionary for Lovers*. It tells the edgy story of a Chinese girl from the countryside who makes her way to London. Z, as the narrator calls herself in London, struggles from the beginning of the story to the end over her love affair with a British hold-over hippy. She struggles with his artist's temperament, she struggles with the concept of love and she struggles with the grammar of the not perfectly translatable words *ài* and "love".

> *"Love," this English word: like other English words it has tense. "Loved" or "will love" or "have loved." All these specific tenses mean Love is time-limited thing. Not infinite. It only exist in particular period of time [sic]. In Chinese, Love is "爱" (ài). It has no tense. No past and future. Love in Chinese means a being, a situation, a circumstance. Love is existence, holding past and future.*[2]

So here was Z, deploring the idea that her ability to love should be confined by the boundaries of time and the tenses of English verbs. And there was Julia, talking about love in cold, practical terms, and actually

---

2   Guo, Xiaolu, *A Concise Chinese-English Dictionary for Lovers*, Doubleday, 2007, p. 239.

punctuating its transitory nature by saying she loved her husband "for now". Two Chinese women whose ideas of modern love were so different, apparently bound up with how they used the word.

Z is right about the grammar of English and Chinese verbs. Chinese verbs are simple; there is a single form of a verb, *ài*, which never changes form for tense like English verbs do (love, loved, loved; sing, sang, sung) or for person (I love, she loves).

Every day in China, I praised the simplicity of Chinese grammar and the absence of the forced march of memorisation, which makes Latin, with its *amo-amas-amat* and the like, notorious – and which makes English, with its irregular and random-seeming verb variations, so hard for foreigners to master. But I also found it disorienting. Verb tense is so second-nature for speakers of most western languages that we hardly notice it; yet we feel unfinished without it. We English speakers use tense to build information about time right into the verb itself. If I say "I sang a song", using the past-tense form of the verb "sing", I mean that this action happened at an earlier point in time. In Chinese, since there is no tense, you instead have to throw in some words of context to indicate time, like yesterday or today or tomorrow. For example, *Zuótiān wǒ chànggē* is literally "Yesterday I sing song".

Chinese can also add a few shades of meaning to a verb with something called aspect. You might use aspect, for example, when you want to stress that the action you're talking about is continuing or ongoing, as opposed to saying something more general.

Here is how it works: say I ask Julia how she helps her child fall asleep at night, she might say that every night she sings a song to her: "*Wǒ chànggē*" or "I sing a song". Very straightforward, nothing going on with aspect. But now imagine the scene where Julia is singing a song to her daughter, the phone rings, it is for her, and she is summoned to talk. She might want to say that she'll call back because she is busy singing a song to her daughter: "*Wǒ zài chànggē*" or "I am singing a song". In this case, she wants to stress that the action is ongoing, and she is engaged in doing it right now. She does that by using the aspect word *zài*. You can think of it as "-ing" in English. Some languages, like Russian and Greek, have very elaborate sets of aspect expressions that add different nuances of meaning. Other languages, like Chinese, have just a few.

Maybe, I thought, these entanglements of tense and aspect and how to use them in a foreign language explained the trouble I was having understanding Julia. Maybe she didn't mean she loved her husband "for now" in a temporary way, but rather she was being more existential, or even more romantic, like "I am in love with my husband". I hoped that was so. But I also know that problems with love go beyond problems of grammar.

Certainly, China's changing concepts of love and marriage have not segued gracefully through the twentieth century. Rather they have lurched along, matching in turbulence the country's changing identities: Confucianism; an East-West Confucian-Christian mélange during the brief Nationalist period; the revolutionary and doctrinaire Communist era; the new "Socialism with Chinese characteristics", which the rest of the world thinks of as capitalism with an authoritarian state. The Confucian tradition of harmonious but strictly regulated love and marriage gave way to Mao's more egalitarian, yet politically correct marriage, followed by a cracking-apart of the old rules, and now circling back to a Confucian revival alongside youthful love-by-choice in the newly affluent era.

When I was out on the streets, looking at the faces of the people I passed, I sometimes tried to guess where they had been as China was cycling through the chaos of the decades of their lives. Had their education halted just as they were entering high school? Had they been sent to the countryside, and how did they return? Were they married for politics, or love, or by arrangement? What did they believe about love and relationships in their day, and do they still believe it now? Different ideas of love and marriage co-exist in China today, albeit not always seamlessly, as I have seen played out in small public dramas.

The cherry blossom spring flower festival this year happened to coincide with the first gloriously warm and clear weekend days of the season. All of Beijing was out of doors after the dank and dreary winter. On Sunday, at Yuyuantan Park on the west side of the city, boys bought their girls sprigs of bright pink and white plastic cherry blossoms, which the girls wound into wreaths and wore in their hair. The lake was crowded with pedal boats, and farmers sold baby chicks and bunnies from cardboard boxes. Everyone was paired off, or so it seemed. Young couples filled the subways and the parks that day, all locked in embrace. They held hands, they hugged, they kissed, they spooned, all mindless or careless of their public display. I would say these are the youth of the marry-for-love generation.

On that same day, had we been in Shanghai's People's Park instead, we would no doubt have again seen the serious matchmaking meetings that we observed there every weekend while we lived in Shanghai. Parents in their fifties, worried about their unmarried offspring in their late twenties, would gather in the northwest corner of the park with their homemade signs describing their children. This son was born in the year of the monkey, was 1.8 metres tall, had a job in a small private company, and was Type A blood. That daughter was a graduate of East China Normal University, was 1.6 metres tall, Type A blood, of Han ethnic group, and her picture was cute.

The parents would circle around tentatively, reading others' posters, huddling with their spouses, and perhaps sidling toward another couple to strike up a conversation and see where things might go from there. The

A matchmaking mother in Shanghai's People ʂ ɪ ark

grown children were never in evidence. (Who knows? They may have been locked in embrace on the Number 2 line subway at that very moment!) These were adults of another era, and were still trying to arrange marriages for their very modern youth.

Maybe love, 爱, is a metaphor for much that is now unfolding and changing in China. One generation, the parents who prowl the park on Sundays matchmaking for their children, is stuck in the old idea of love, while another generation, Julia and Z, is testing new definitions of love. China is betwixt and between on many issues, of which one is love.

Bú yào! Don't want, don't need!

Chapter 2

When rude is polite

MY FIRST LANGUAGE school in China was called Miracle Mandarin. I chose it partly for its jaunty name and partly for its location. Miracle Mandarin held classes in a traditional lane house (Americans would call it a row house), tucked into a small quiet alley in one of Shanghai's 1920s-style neighbourhoods. During breaks between classes, we students would stand outside for some fresh air and if we were lucky, a sliver of sunshine. The Europeans would all have a smoke. We would watch the comings and goings in the alley: old men emerged for their daily exercise, old women headed off to shop. Once, we watched a family move out of their lane house. For three days, men on tricycle carts came to take away boxes, bedding, cabinets and chairs. Then, carrying everything on their backs, they hauled out the refrigerator, cupboards, a sink, and finally stacks and stacks of wooden boards and frames. They seemed to be

dismantling the entire internal structure of the house, loading it onto their tricycles and riding away.

Each morning, I would trace the same path to and from my school. Just before ten o'clock in the morning, I crossed a dozen lanes of traffic under the busy overpass of Chengdu Road and continued up Nanjing Road past the buildings of the Shanghai TV station. Every day just after one o'clock, I retraced my steps home.

Day after day, then week after week, my route took me past the same group of young guys who were selling knock-off goods on the sidewalk. "Lady! Lady! You buy my bag! Come look my warehouse! I have Gucci! I have Prada!"

Each time, I dutifully slowed down, engaged for a moment, then declined the offers with a string of *Bú yào. Bú yào. Bú yào.* "Don't want. Don't want. Don't want." I figure that some degree of tolerance is the personal duty I owe as a foreign guest in the country. After so many passages, I knew each hawker well enough to tell who had got a new haircut. They never seemed to recognise me. I was just another mark.

Finally, one day I had enough. I snapped, and dug for my new vocabulary. "*Zuótiān, bú yào! Jīntiān bú yào!*

Míngtiān bú yào!" I shouted back. "Yesterday, don't want! Today, don't want! Tomorrow, don't want!"

They stopped cold, stunned. Then one irrepressible soul quickly recovered, and with a plaintive look whispered earnestly "*Hòutiān?*" meaning "Day after tomorrow?"

I actually felt pretty pleased with myself. It's always great when what you study in the classroom works on the street. But I also felt pretty rude when I yelled out a blunt-seeming "Don't want!" I know *bú yào* is what Chinese people themselves would say, but it still felt abrupt.

In fact, I often feel like I'm being abrupt and blunt, and even rude when I'm speaking Chinese. *Bú yào* (don't want), *bú yòng* (don't need), *méi yǒu* (don't have) *bú shì* (is not) *bù kěyǐ* (cannot) – all these are standard forms of declining offers or requests or saying no. But each time I use them, I fight the urge to pad them with a few niceties like thank you, excuse me or I'm sorry.

Blunt is what I hear back from the Chinese as well, but from them it does not seem intended as rude. It is just what it is. Here are some classic scenes from my everyday life:

> *Passengers inside jam-packed subway cars jostle and yell "Xià chē!", "Off the car!" There is no "Excuse me", "pardon me" or "sorry" to be heard.*

*In any public place, a mobile phone rings and someone screams the greeting "*Wèi!*", a response that reaches the decibel level of a yell of FIRE! in a crowded theatre.*

"Fúwùyuán! Fúwùyuán!" or "Waitress! Waitress!" diners cry to demand a glass, a bowl, or a pair of chopsticks. And no "Miss, could you please get me another beer?"

That is the etiquette of the street. On a more intimate level, the grammar of politeness is equally complex. On the one hand, the people in China can be effortlessly gentle and courteous. Take, for instance, the Beijing tradition of *màn zŏu. Màn* means "slowly", and *zŏu* means "walk", or together "walk slowly". *Màn zŏu* is the tender goodbye offered from every small shopkeeper I have visited in Beijing. It is usually spoken in a quiet voice, and somehow sounds so much more sincere than "Have a nice day". Sometimes, I would make the trip to my neighbourhood laundry with a single shirt for cleaning, just as an excuse to hear the *màn zŏu* when I left the shop.

At the same time, among good friends, the contrasts between the politesse of what you do and the bluntness of what you say can seem baffling. At a restaurant with friends, a delicate choreography will have one person carefully select a few choice morsels from the common bowl and place them on a neighbour's plate. It is a small, perfect gesture. Another person will pour tea or beer for everyone else before even considering pouring his own. And then, another will announce *"Gěi wǒ yán!"*, literally, "Give me salt!" with no sign of a please or thank you involved. I'm always taken a little aback and, after so many years of training children in western table manners, bite my tongue to stifle a "Say please!".

My Chinese friends say they notice that Westerners use lots of pleases (*qǐng*) and thank yous (*xièxie*) when speaking Chinese. And actually, they say, we use way too many of them for Chinese taste. A Chinese linguist, Kaidi Zhan, says that using a please as in "Please pass the salt" actually has the opposite effect of politeness here in China. The Chinese way of being polite to each other with words is to shorten the social distance between you. And saying please serves to insert a kind of buffer or space that says, in effect, that we need some formality between us here.[3] One of my tutors, a young guy named Danny, who straddles the line between being a Chinese nationalist and an edgy global youth, nodded his head enthusiastically when I asked him about this interpretation: "Good friends are so close, they are like part of you," Danny said. "Why would you say please or thank you to yourself? It doesn't make sense."

3   Zhan, Kaidi, *The Strategies of Politeness in the Chinese Language*, Institute of East Asian Studies, University of California, Berkeley, 1992.

Certainly, Chinese verbal courtliness is minimal compared with Japanese, where foreign language learners struggle to weave in the "I so kindly request" and "from my lowly position I ask" grace notes that make up about half of every Japanese sentence. One of my random discoveries about the rudimentary, if effective, nature of Chinese manners was about a particularly grating sound that drove me crazy for the year and a half living in our apartment building in Beijing.

Every employee in our apartment building had a walkie-talkie. There must have been a rule to keep them on, with volume turned up to the max at all times. These were the old-fashioned walkie-talkies, the kind where the talker screams into his end, and the noise comes screeching out of the other end like the cackle of angry crows. The halls of our building sounded like a radio dispatch room for New York taxis.

The oddity about the walkie-talkie language is that every broadcast ends with a drawn-out vowel, sounding like "aaahh". The quality is so garbled that I only ever caught a few words. I guess they were saying things like "Plumbing problem in 2105! Will you go check it out – aaahh?" Or "Lots of noise on floor 8. Will you see what's going on – aaahh?" All day long, there was a barrage of all these calls and replies, all ending with a loud aaahh.

Then one day, I was thumbing through one of my Chinese grammar books, and I found something that unlocked the mystery. What I had thought was some horrible and annoying tic is actually a common way of being polite. When you add the particle "a" at the end of an expression, you actually lessen the punch and soften your delivery. The walkie-talkie dispatchers are being nicer to each other by adding all those aaahhs to their speech, serving much the same purpose as the qualifiers "could", "would" and "might" in English. The "Will you see what's going on aaahh?" is understood as the more polite "*Could* you see what's going on?"

I stumbled upon an even more delightful discovery in the so-called dirt market on Beijing's south side. Foreigners and tourists throng to the weekend market, but the locals do, too. A Chinese woman visiting from Guangzhou, the former Canton, who went with me one day, said she really has no idea why the Chinese love this market. So, we headed for the aisles most crowded with Chinese people to see what they liked to buy.

The aisles with Chinese shoppers were crammed with jade of all sorts – bracelets, amulets and beads. There were piles of petrified-looking walnuts, rubbed to a gleaming, lacquered shine. Men squatted down to examine the patterns of the shells and tried rolling them around in their hands like giant worry-beads. There were strange horns of animals, polished gems of agate or lapis and simple river stones in varying shapes.

Always on the lookout for occasional one-off items, a piece of jewellery or a jar that I like to imagine came from someone's farmhouse in the countryside, I stopped at a stall with a collection of pretty blue stones. Maybe they were lapis, but maybe they were just lovely glass. The vendor had made some pieces into pendants and others into rings with silver bands. "*Zuò zuò*," she said to me, pulling out a miniature stool when I lingered.

There it was: *zuò zuò*. I understood immediately. She was not just saying "sit", but something more polite like "Just have a seat for a few minutes". I had stumbled upon the double verb and was instantly smitten. Linguists can split hairs about the real effect of doubling the verb: that the action will be short, e.g. *xiū xiū* = take a little rest; or is minimal in importance, e.g. *máfan máfan nǐ* = bother you just a little; or makes a statement tentative, e.g. *xiū xiū shì shì*, literally fix fix try try, which would mean something like "have a try at fixing" something. The point is that in all these cases, doubling the verb (or the variant form, breaking up the doubled words with *yi* as in *kàn yi kàn*) softens its impact.

I now double my verbs at every opportunity, partly because it is fun, and partly because I feel gentler and more polite when I do it. I discovered that if I say *kàn kàn* or *kàn yi kàn* to shop girls, "I'm just looking; I'll just have a look; I'm looking around", they would back off instantly, and let me look in peace. It works like magic.

I've expanded to a host of other double verbs:

Shì shì mǎ *(try try + question)* "Can I just try it on?" I say this when I want to try on the goods, but make no commitments.

Zǒu zǒu *(walk walk)* "I'm out for a little walk." I say this to aggressive pedicab drivers looking for a fare.

Wánr wánr *(play play)* "We're just having a little fun and relaxation!" I say this when I'm telling people we're just going out for no particular reason.

It was a perfect day at the dirt market. When I left, the shop girl who let me *zuò zuò* on her small stool said gently, "*Màn zǒu.*"

狮 十 使 是

Shī, Shí, Shǐ, Shì   Lion, ten, to make, to be

Chapter 3

Language play as a national sport

IF I COULD time travel, I would go back about a century and look for a man named Chao Yuen Ren 赵元任. I first heard of Chao,[4] a writer and scholar, from an old China hand and language buff. "If you ever find anything by Chao Yuen Ren," he told me, "buy it. His books are hard to find, but well worth the search."

Pictures of Chao in his early twenties capture a baby-faced young man, with round spectacles and a shock of suave combed-back hair, looking very dapper in a western suit and tie. His clothes look a

---

4   I have seen Chao Yuen Ren also written as Zhao Yuanren. Chao Yuen Ren is written in the Wade-Giles romanisation system, which was popular in China from the late nineteenth century through most of the twentieth century. Zhao Yuanren is the rendering in the romanisation system of Pinyin, which was introduced in China in 1958, later adopted internationally, and is still used today. I have chosen the Wade-Giles form here, as I first heard of him as Chao Yuen Ren, and his name appears that way in the books I own that were written by him.

tad large for him, as if they might have been rented for the photo session, which is the practice of brides and grooms in today's China. Chao was something of a Renaissance man, shuttling back and forth between the great universities of America and China throughout his life, which spanned nearly the whole twentieth century, as a mathematician, philosopher, musician and linguist. He composed pop Chinese music,[5] and wrote grammars and dictionaries; his wife, a physician named Yang Buwei, wrote about Chinese cuisine.

Chao designed an early version of a way to render the Chinese language in the Roman alphabet so that it could be read phonetically. He also made up a system for writing tones, and – showing a window into his very playful soul – he translated Lewis Carroll's *Jabberwocky* and *Alice's Adventures in Wonderland* into Chinese. Yet after all this, he is probably best known in China for a story about a lion-eating poet, which is composed of 92 characters, each one pronounced the same way: *shi* (sounds like sure in English).[6]

---

5 Here is a link (all links are current at the time of printing) to a recording of his song, "How could I help thinking of her" (教我如何不想她 jiāo wǒ rúhé bù xiǎng tā) which sounds most like a languorous cowboy's campfire song. http://v.youku.com/v_playlist/f1286025o1p4.html

6 The variants of *shi* are pronounced with different tones, but even so …

Discovering his story was vindication for me: I always had the impression that Chinese "all sounds the same", and here was proof! Chao's story is 92 repetitions of the

Chao Yuen Ren

syllable *shi*. It is perfectly understandable if you read the characters silently, by sight. But if you read those characters out loud, there are 92 "sures" in a row.

"The Lion-Eating Poet in the Stone Den" is the story of a poet (*shī*) named Shi who loves to eat lions (*shí shī*), goes to the market (*shì*) to buy ten (*shí*) of them,

31

石室詩士施氏
嗜獅　誓食十獅
氏時時適市視獅
十時　適十獅適市
是時　適施氏適市
氏視是十獅　恃矢勢
使是十獅逝世
氏拾是十獅屍　適石室
石室濕　氏使侍拭石室
石室拭　氏始試食是十獅屍
食時　始識是十獅屍
實十石獅屍
試釋是事

The Lion-Eating Poet

takes them home to eat (*shi*) and discovers they are made (*shǐ*) of stone (*shi*).

Such language play works because the Chinese sound system uses only about 400 syllables, compared to 4000 in English. So, there are lots of syllables, like *shi*, that have multiple meanings.

The syllables of Chinese are really simple, just a consonant and a vowel, like *nǐ, hǎo, ma, kuài, chī, fàn*. A few syllables end in what linguists consider a part-vowel/half-consonant of n, r or ng. These are simple when compared with more complex syllables in English with its strings of consonants, like streets, cramp, blast, crafts. Words in Chinese are mostly either one syllable long, like *shi*, or two, like *mǐfàn*. The latter are usually compound words, two little ones put together, comparable to breakwall, upstart, or firefly. English, by contrast, is laden with complicated multi-syllable words like fortitude, reasoning ... on up to antidisestablishmentarianism.

When I described this Chinese word structure to my sister, she commented, quite rightly, "So, Chinese is not so great for playing Scrabble."

The Chinese may not play Scrabble, but they do play with their language a lot, handling their small inventory of syllables quite preciously, like Fabergé eggs, to see how much curious potential they can discover in each one.

The more I picked up of the Chinese language going on around me, the more it seemed to me that the typical Chinese person was keenly invested in his own language, whether for fun or as a serious pursuit. The Chinese revere their language for its history, which has often been political and is reflected even in varying names for the Chinese language. It is called *Pǔtōnghuà*, or "common speech", and *Hànyǔ*, or "the Han people's language", or *Zhōngwén*, or "the Chinese language", and other names as well. And everyone has to make a lifelong effort to learn the characters and then maintain a working command of them, so the language and its complications are always on their minds. They both goof around with the language and fear it for its superstitious power.

Because of its spare syllable structure, Chinese offers a heyday for punsters, jokesters, storytellers, bloggers, twitterers and other language mavens. One form of rapid-fire comedy dialogue, much like Abbott and Costello or maybe the old radio talk show comedians, George Burns and Gracie Allen, is called *xiàngsheng* 相声 or "crosstalk". I can't follow a word of any crosstalk I hear, but I love watching the Chinese react to it. At my neighbourhood laundry in Beijing, the skinny man who ironed shirts with a massive, heavy, industrial-strength iron that looked like a pre-war relic, always had a TV playing in the background. He usually cocked one ear to the dour daily soaps, which favour hospital scenes, a family figure fading away, and others weeping quietly in the background. But when *xiàngsheng* aired, as it always does during the long Chinese New Year holidays, the laundry man was at attention, laughing uproariously, forgetting about his iron. I never left anything for ironing during that season, for risk of burnmarks.

The Chinese are very superstitious about their language. They consider the number 4 unlucky, like 13 in the west. I couldn't tell you why 13 is unlucky, but every Chinese can tell you that 4 is unlucky because the word for the number "four", *sì* 四, sounds like the word for "die", *sǐ* 死. People go to great lengths to avoid using four. There is nary a 4th or 14th or 24th floor in any high-rise building. I always looked for, but only very rarely saw, a licence plate or even a telephone number containing the number 4.

Conversely, people pay lots of money to secure a licence plate or a phone number with the digit 8, because eight, *bā* 八, rhymes with *fā* as in *fā cái*, which means "to become wealthy" in Mandarin. The power of 8 drove the opening of the Beijing Olympics into the rainy season, just so they could begin on the auspicious 08/08/08 at 8:08. (It didn't rain.)

Similarly, you should never give a clock as a wedding present, because the word for "clock", *zhōng* 钟, sounds the same as the word for "end", *zhōng* 终, which might suggest the end of the relationship. And at Chinese New Year, you should hang the banner with the symbol for *fú* 福 or "good fortune" upside down beside your doorway, because the word *dào* means both "to arrive" and "upside down". Hence hanging good fortune (*fú*) 福 upside down (*dào*) also means good fortune (*fú*) 福 will arrive (*dào*) at your doorstep in the coming year. This may seem like a stretch, but the practice is very popular!

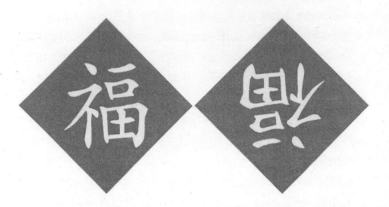

Fú, "good fortune", right side up and upside down

Internet punsters are famous for hiding meanings behind their seemingly innocent online postings when they want to avoid being caught by the political censors. One modern fable – which punned as a story about the Communist Party – spread like wildfire across the internet in early 2009.

On its surface, this concocted "grass-mud horse" fable was innocent enough. It was a story about a horse that lived in the desert, under a threat from invasion of river crabs. But the puns of the words told a very different story, one about the march of Party censorship on the internet. When net users (called "netizens" in China) read the characters aloud, the puns were obvious, and the meaning of the story became radically different.

Chinese love idioms, proverbs, sayings and morals of the story. They have particular esteem for four-character sayings that sum up a story or fable; others make a historical reference or evoke classics, and others are offered as a nugget of wisdom from everyday life. *Chéngyǔ*, the most classical of the four-character set phrases, are studied in school. They are cherished as linguistic treasures, far more than their English counterparts are, like "the boy who cried wolf" or to "cross the Rubicon" or "a Trojan horse".

My teacher Danny taught me one: *shǒu zhū dài tù* 守株待兔, which means "sitting by a stump, waiting for a rabbit". It is really an evocation of a lazy person who waits for a handout instead of working for a living. The back story is about a guy lazing under a tree one day, when suddenly a rabbit hops along and runs right into the tree, knocking itself out. "Dinner!" thinks the lazy guy, who goes home to make rabbit stew. He returns the next day, and maybe every day afterwards, to sit under the tree and wait expectantly for another rabbit to present itself as dinner, instead of going out trying to earn his own keep.

It was hard to work "sitting by a stump waiting for a rabbit" into my conversations, but I did manage to use a little language play of my own one day. I had learned the phrase *xiàn xué xiàn mài*, literally "now study now sell" or colloquially, to "use on the spot what you have just learned; teaching something that you only just now learned yourself". I tried this out on a friend of mine while we were driving along a busy Beijing street in a taxi. The story I was relating wasn't funny, but the taxi driver, listening in, burst out laughing, giving me pause to imagine that I sounded like a pre-schooler with a bad knock-knock joke, and that as a foreigner, I should attempt language play judiciously.

The flip side to all the fun and games of Chinese is ambiguity. With so many sounds that have multiple meanings, there is a frequent need to clarify. Context works sometimes, but not always, not by any means.

My favourite way out of this is what I call the "B as in Bob" phenomenon. For example, sometimes when talking on the phone in English, it's hard to distinguish between the sounds for "s" and "f". If context isn't enough to sort out the confusion, you can seek clarification by saying "S as in Sam", or "F as in France".

The Chinese use this, too, with whole syllables. Say there is a word in Chinese, like *xīn*, which I know means "new" 新. I hear the word *xīn* used in a context where it can't sensibly mean "new", so I might ask the speaker, "*Xīnnián de xīn?*" (new as in new year). He might respond, No, "*kāi xīn de xīn*" (heart as in "open heart", which means "happy") where *xīn* 心 means "heart" and *kāi xīn* means "happy". With all the struggles endured in learning Chinese, I enjoy this cheap thrill of using language like an insider.

If I could write and read characters well, I would also try the visual approach to disambiguating. The Chinese write tiny characters for each other to read on scraps of paper, if they're trying to identify a homonym. Or they draw characters with a finger in the air.

So back to the prolific Chao Yuen Ren and my ongoing search for his books. I did find a few of them. One was the best Chinese grammar that I have come across, written in 1968. The other is a collection of pieces on Chinese language, including his charming linguistic autobiography, in which Chao recounts a lifelong habit of picking up a variety of languages and Chinese dialects. What I continue to love about this man is his fearless Chinese approach to his own language, as something to be both admired and enjoyed.

Dǎbāo Do you do take-away?

Chapter 4

Why the Chinese hear tones, and we don't

AFTER SEVERAL MONTHS in China, I developed a bad craving for cheese, which is a precious and hard-to-find luxury in the highly lactose-intolerant nation. Desperate, I stopped in a Taco Bell at the fringe of swanky downtown Shanghai, fixed on the idea of a gooey, sloppy, cheesy burrito.

A tall Chinese youth, proudly wearing a black sombrero and sequined velvet waistcoat, greeted me at the entrance. He barked a hearty *"Huānyíng guānglín!"*

We welcome you! Any restaurant in China worth its salt will post brigades of enthusiastic greeters at the door. They're usually lovely young women dressed in traditional *qípáo* with a thigh-high slit up the side. But at Taco Bell, it was boys in oversized sombreros.

I decided on take-away. China has wholly embraced the culture of take-away food and even better, of doggy bags for restaurant leftovers. After another oversized Chinese feast at just about any eatery from the humble to the most glorious, the evening's host will head home bearing carefully packaged Styrofoam boxes, *dǎbāo*, for the family's next meal.

Still quite new to China, I had rehearsed my lines to ask for the menu and inquire about take-away. "*Yǒu dǎbāo ma?*" "Do you have take-away?"

When the greeter in the sombrero looked puzzled, I asked again, pointing to the menu, then the door, and miming the act of carrying a bag out the entrance. Still no response.

I cut out the grammar and said simply "*Dǎbāo?*", "Take-away?" Nothing.

Then I tried all sorts of tones on the two syllables of *dabao*: high tones, rising tones, falling tones, falling-then-rising tones and various combinations thereof. All the time I'm thinking: "C'mon, guy! Work with me here! How hard can this be?"

He called for reinforcements from the kitchen. Several more young boys in sombreros emerged, listened intently as I repeated *dabao* over and over again. Finally, one erupted in triumph, "Aaahh – *dǎbāo!*", this uttered with a very emphatic high tone on the *bāo*. The greeter solemnly answered, "*Yǒu*" ("We have it"). And then they all laughed and went back into the kitchen.

Tones: such a thorn in the side of students of Chinese. But tones actually serve a clever purpose. Since

Mandarin has an inventory of only about 400 syllables, about a tenth of English, the language is simply flooded with homonyms – words that sound alike but have different meanings. English has homonyms, too, like "seal", meaning the animal, the stamp or the verb to close tightly. But Mandarin has literally countless homonyms, which makes for a lot of ambiguity.

Tones are a way to get a lot more mileage out of each syllable. If you slap a rising tone onto a syllable, it has one meaning; if you pronounce that same syllable with a falling tone, it means something else.[7] Here are just some of the possible meanings for *bao* that the boy in the sombrero may have *heard and understood* when I tried saying *dabao* using several different tones at the Taco Bell:

Bāo 包 *with the first tone, a high tone, means "bag" or "parcel" as a noun, and "to wrap up" as a verb. (*Dǎbāo 打包*, the two-syllable word, means "carry-out" or "take-away").*

Báo 雹 *with the second, rising tone means "hail", as in the frozen rain pellets.*

---

7 Even after the variations for tone, there are still lots of homonyms in Chinese. Many syllables spoken with the same tone – exactly identical to the ear – have different meanings. They are usually represented by different characters in the writing system.

Bǎo 饱 *with the third tone, falling then rising, means you have "eaten your fill".*

Bào 报 *with the fourth, or falling tone, means "a newspaper". And* bào 抱 *also means "to hug or embrace".*

Who knows, with all these versions of *bao*, and just as many for *da*, I may have been asking that boy for anything from a newspaper to a big hug.

Taco Bell in Chinese

English speakers may be surprised to hear this, but English actually has tones, too. Tones in English don't change the meaning of a word like they do in Chinese, but they can change the meaning of a whole phrase or sentence.

You'll recognise this: if you say "We have to gó?" with a rising tone at the end of the sentence, the meaning of the whole sentence is understood as a question.

If, by contrast, you say "We have to go" with no tone or "We have to gò" with a falling tone on "go", the sentence is understood as just a statement. (Stress also adds nuance to the meaning; if you put a lot of stress on the word "go", you add a sense of urgency.)

If you answer the question "Do we have to go?" with a simple "No", you can play with tones to shade the meaning of your answer, too. A falling tone on "nò" is pretty straightforward. But if you pronounce "nǒ" with a falling-then-rising tone (like the third tone in Chinese, which seems to have a kind of gravelly-sounding pause at the bottom of the dip), it means something more like "No, but ... " as though there could be consequences or complications in not going.

Knowing this helps outsiders understand *about* tones, but it doesn't help us much in actually hearing tones and pronouncing them. Mastering tones shouldn't be as hard as in practice it seems to be; there is no physiological or linguistic reason for tones to be so difficult. In fact, more languages of the world use tones than don't. And many have more tones than Mandarin does; Cantonese has seven tones; Vietnamese and Thai have five.

But mastering tones *is* hard. The only tone in Mandarin that I can easily recognise in daily chatter is the high tone, because it is so distinctive. One friend, a teacher, told me that the high tone is a dead giveaway of a foreigner's accent; she said the key to pronouncing the tone right is to hold the high pitch steady, and not let it slide off at the end. "Think of it musically," she said, "like the mi of do-re-mi. Just aim for mi and hold it there."

Hearing and saying the tones is one thing; remembering which tone goes with which meaning is quite another. Tones are just one more arbitrary thing to learn about Chinese, similar to the inflections of Latin verbs (*amo, amas, amat*), the genders of French nouns (*le chapeau, la vie*), or the honorifics of Japanese.

For the first year or so of studying Chinese, I asked lots of people – Chinese teachers, new students, bilingual China hands – for their tricks for remembering which tones to use. I received a creative collection of responses.

First came the Vivid Colours method for learning tones. This is fun in a parlour game kind of way. First you assign each tone a colour. Then as you learn each new word, you visualise it in that colour. Artsy types, and those with a Zen-like nature, do well with this method.

I chose a palette of neon Technicolour, inspired by the bright neon lights that dress up Shanghai buildings at night. These assignments seemed intuitive to me: neon green for a rising tone; red for a falling tone; bright yellow like the sun for a high tone; and blue like the waves in the sea for a falling-rising tone.

My system broke down when I could not remember which colour I had assigned to which word. And worse, sometimes the meaning of the word was counter-intuitive with the colour. Take red, for example. *Hóng* (red) is an important word in China. Red channels good fortune, happiness, and it is symbolic of China as a nation. *Hóng bāo*, red envelopes, are given as gifts at celebrations; brides wear red; red is east; and red is the colour of China's flag. Chinese women look particularly good wearing red. In my system, I gave red a falling tone, because I think of a stop sign. Unfortunately, *hóng* actually has a rising tone.

So next came the Full Body method. My Chinese teacher Sandy excelled at this. Sandy, like most of my teachers, was in her early twenties. She had fled the rural provinces for a better life in the east-coast cities, studied at college to teach Chinese as a foreign language, and could talk anyone under the table with her mastery of present perfect progressives ("I have been singing") or resultative adjectives with postpositive placement ("Iron the clothes dry" where "dry" is the result of ironing).

Sandy uncorked energy during class. Day after day, week after week, Sandy went aerobic – up on her tiptoes for a high tone; deep knee bends with a falling tone; an upward sweep of her arms for a rising tone; a spritely curtsy for the falling-rising tone. She would not fail us; we would master tones!

This method resonated with some of my fellow students, who practised the anaerobic version, wagging their fingers or arms like a music conductor as they spoke. We were a fidgety class.

I found one word where this method worked particularly well: *yóuyǒng* (rising, then falling-rising tone) means "swim". As opposed to *yǒuyòng* (falling-rising, then falling tone), meaning "useful". I visualised swimming as the arc of the arm rising out of the water (*yóu* = rising tone) then down for the stroke and back up again (*yǒng* = falling-then-rising tone). But this system doesn't scale well; it was a lot of work for just one word and was finally exhausting.

Some of my classmates tried the Drinking model. During my graduate school days studying linguistics in America, we widely accepted the theory that a few beers stripped away linguistic inhibitions, loosening the tongue and accelerating mastery of foreign languages. In China, Tsingdao beers at the local *jiǔ bā*, or "bar", served that purpose.

The best time to approach tones, of course, would be at birth. Ah, to be born Chinese and have this all come naturally. But with the good news of effortless tone mastery comes a bit of bad news: Chinese speakers have a hard time *not* hearing tones. That is, for Chinese speakers, tones are so integral that they can't separate the sounds of the word from the tone of the word.

For example, if a foreigner doesn't pronounce the tone correctly (like me with *dǎbāo*), a typical Chinese person (boy in sombrero) would have a hard time making the leap to imagine what in the world the foreigner was trying to say. It just wouldn't occur to him that someone might be saying the word "take-away" when he was hearing the word "hug". Any more than it would occur to an English speaker that a foreigner might be saying, "I was out in Beijing, and I saw no crowds anywhere!" when he was actually saying, "I was out in Beijing, and I saw no clouds anywhere!"

Tones are sometimes even a problem among the Chinese talking to each other. Although speakers of the Sichuan dialect and of standard Mandarin can understand each other pretty well, they wrestle over the tones, which are different. In Sichuanese, the third and fourth tones are reversed from those of Mandarin.

One Chinese woman, who was fluent in English, told me that her attachment to tones caused a real problem for her when she was learning English. She explained that she was taught English vocabulary in a very rote way, word by word, with each new word pronounced with a falling tone. The students would recite lists: hàt, stòp, etc. She said she had to consciously force herself to make the tone on a word rise at the end of the sentence, as when making a question. For example, if she had to say, "Do you like my hát?" with a rising tone on hat to indicate the question, she could hardly do it. "I knew I was supposed to raise the tone, but I didn't know how to do it," she said.

Every foreigner struggling to learn Chinese has humbling and classic trouble-with-tones stories like mine with *dǎbāo*. (I can only imagine how the Chinese relate their versions of these stories!) As one friend summed up the situation: the poor foreigners yammer away with tones all bollixed up so the words and the message remain utterly unintelligible to the Chinese. There must be a metaphor here, he suggested, for the gap between what we think we're saying and what the Chinese are actually hearing.[8]

And I think he's right. I think it's a metaphor for the fragility of how we and the Chinese are getting acquainted. We stumble along toward each other, well-intentioned, I would say, and generally moving forward. But we can unwittingly run smack into a gaffe that flusters our perceptions and interpretations of a situation (the Dalai Lama? The Uighurs? Visas? Swine flu? Trade agreements?) or each other. How could we all be so wrong? The moral here: foreigners should pay attention to tones, and the Chinese should learn to imagine words without the proper tone.

---

8   Thanks to Orville Schell.

老百姓

Lǎobǎixìng   Common folk

Chapter 5

China's Ordinary Joe

WHEN WE FIRST moved to China, I would fight to escape crowds, seeking out the quiet alleyways or at least the less-crowded side of the street. It is difficult to avoid a crowd in a country of 1.3 billion people. Crowds gather to exercise in the parks even at the earliest hours of the morning. At noontime, queues swell in front of the best dumpling or steamed-bun stands. On trendy city streets, day crowds of office workers meld into night crowds of shoppers who browse the vendors' sidewalk blankets spread thick with cheap jewellery or hair clips in summer, and gloves or warm socks in winter. Crowds beget crowds beget crowds.

Then one day I learned about the value of crowds. I was standing nearly alone at a corner crossing; there were just two of us pedestrians. As I stepped off the kerb onto a one-way street, with oncoming traffic stopped 30 yards to my right and the green walk sign blinking in my favour, from the left shot a motor scooter – which hit me and knocked me to the ground. I was bruised and bloody, my shoes and books scattered. The scooter driver was immediately long gone. After that day, I shifted allegiance and sought the centre and safety of crowds. I embraced any crowd of *lǎobǎixìng* – the common folk, ordinary people, the average Chinese Joe – that I encountered.

Lǎobǎixìng: one of the first words foreigners latch on to; it's easy to hear and easy to say. *Lǎobǎixìng* 老百姓. Lao – by – shing: three long, languorous syllables, standing out among so many strings of short, choppy words.

I overheard it in conversations on subways and elevators, or as I passed old men chatting on park benches. It popped out from the drone of talk radio inside taxis or on the TV news, describing mobbed train stations or the hordes at gala openings of new shopping malls or at holiday temple fairs. *Lǎobǎixìng* was right there, entrenched in the middle of normal, everyday, chaotic, crowded life in China.

Lǎo + *bǎi* + *xìng* literally means "old" + "hundred" + "names". In Chinese it has become a shortcut to convey the sense of "everybody", since most of the Chinese population share the same family names. Indeed, today, some 85% of Chinese people share only 100 such names. Imagine the implications.

The dictionary definition, "common folk, ordinary people", is pretty good, but it feels far too sterile.

Lǎobǎixìng is one of those words where you need to get a feeling through stories or experiences to understand the gist.

Other languages have words like this, words that carry a lot of baggage: *citoyen* during the French Revolution, *Volk* in Hitler's Germany. When John F. Kennedy stood at the Berlin Wall in 1963 and said "*Ich bin ein Berliner*," the world knew exactly what he meant, which was much more than simply a person who happens to live in Berlin.

So it is with *lǎobǎixìng*. Being a *lǎobǎixìng* is much more than being a common or ordinary person. And early on in my time in China, I decided that understanding *lǎobǎixìng* was vital to understanding something of the inner life of the Chinese. I set out to learn what it meant. Who are the *lǎobǎixìng*? Where do you find them? How do they behave? What do they want?

I polled everyone I saw, asking them to tell me who they think the *lǎobǎixìng* are. Here is a sampling of what I found.

A Chinese academic told me, "A *lǎobǎixìng* is anyone but a high Party official." A young Beijing city woman told me that *lǎobǎixìng* is almost everyone in China, except the very politically powerful and maybe very famous people. A veteran American diplomat and a seasoned French businessman both told me wearily, "A *lǎobǎixìng* is just an ordinary person."

"Can rich people be *lǎobǎixìng*?" I pressed. Some respondents said yes, and others said no. What about professors or doctors or entrepreneurs? Same mixed response. One Chinese friend who really got into this line of questioning elaborated that *lǎobǎixìng* themselves would not consider a movie star to be a *lǎobǎixìng*, but a movie star would probably consider herself to be one.

There was consensus on one point: when I asked people if I could be a *lǎobǎixìng*, the response was quick and unanimous, "No, you are not a *lǎobǎixìng*."

Through Chinese history, *lǎobǎixìng* has always referred to the have-nots, rather than the haves. And the focus on what the have-nots lack has shifted through China's political, economic and social upheavals. In dynastic times, it was about having (or not) the power to rule: there were the emperors and imperial people, and there were the *lǎobǎixìng*. During the Cultural Revolution, the term was political; there were Mao's political insiders, and there were the *lǎobǎixìng*. Now, it is economic. Bloggers rant on this theme: "*Lǎobǎixìng*: the common folk; the *People* in the People's Republic of China; the cab drivers, office workers, migrant workers, small shopkeepers, beauticians, food sellers, the people on the street. In essence, it's all those who are trying to make the staggering adjustments to survive ... "[9]

---

9   http://rudenoon.com/absalletc/archives/27

In some circumstances, the word *lǎobǎixìng* is conspicuously avoided. At the showcase military parade in honour of the 60th anniversary of the PRC, President Hu Jintao deliberately invoked the Party-speak of the Maoist era, bypassing *lǎobǎixìng* for the culturally laden period word *tóngzhì*. Standing tall through the open roof of his big black limousine, Hu inched along the parade route and cried out to one flank after another of starched and precise troops, "*TONGZHIMEN HAO!* 同志们好" "COMRADES, GREETINGS!"

Tóngzhì (and its plural *tóngzhìmen*) is bluntly "comrade", and it is now usually only heard either in formal Communist Party-talk, among some of the older generation who are stuck in the past, or on the cutting edge of new China, where *tóngzhì* is code for gay.

I wish I had learned all this earlier; the first Chinese book I studied before we left for China was a 1984 edition, *New Chinese 300*, which liberally invoked *tóngzhì* as a general term of address. So, I went around Shanghai in our early weeks greeting everyone I met with this old word *tóngzhì*, which was heard either as a die-hard Communist throw-back or as new-age ultra-hip slang. I had no idea what I was doing.

I wondered how I could get beyond the word and the definition of *lǎobǎixìng* to the nuances of how they live and what they want. Perhaps I could poke around the edges of *lǎobǎixìng* life and try to mingle my life with theirs. I thought my best shot for getting any traction was at a venue where we naturally mixed, an everyday kind of place where the *lǎobǎixìng* were prevalent and where I could feel comfortable. What better place than shopping? I set out to shop with the *lǎobǎixìng*; I would shop where they shopped and buy what they bought.

My first discovery about *lǎobǎixìng* shopping was clear: the importance of a good deal. Everyone loves a good deal, and *lǎobǎixìng* really love one. There is a drugstore in Hunan Province, in the middle of China, named Laobaixing Drugstore. The chain is billed as the "pricekiller" of drug retailing.[10] On the opening day of a new Wuhan city Laobaixing Drugstore, the store was mobbed by 20,000 people, *lǎobǎixìng* shoppers, who smashed the glass doors in their eagerness to reach the bargain-basement-priced products.

This rang true to me. Shopping at our local Wal-Mart in Beijing (which is not like any Wal-Mart you may have seen elsewhere in the world; it truly caters to the Chinese taste, with touches like duck carcasses hanging from hooks and tanks full of live turtles and carp, for dinner), I saw raucous fisticuffs break out among the Chinese shoppers over the free giveaway shopping bags. In an extreme example of *lǎobǎixìng* shopping from late 2007, a crowd stormed a Carrefour grocery store in Chongqing for a 20% discount on cooking oil, and killed three people. To be fair, I read a similar report

---

10 http://tiny.cc/FZwLI

Lǎobǎixìng **shopping at Wal-Mart in Shanghai**

about a year later about a stampede over pre-Christmas discounts on digital cameras at a Wal-Mart on Long Island, which ended in the death of a store employee.

Such shopping behaviour is partly about a good deal. But, as I learned on my own, it is also driven by the urge to simply get what you can. It is possible to find lots of things in China if you look hard enough and have enough money to buy them. But for *lǎobǎixìng*, the daily fare is thin. I soon found that my regular list of staples, the things I always needed and could count on finding, had shrunk to four: peanuts, yoghurt, Tsingdao beer and whatever jars of jam or the like were not more than six months beyond their supposed expiration date (my self-imposed standard). My former list included more items, but the melamine scandal, bird-flu outbreak, and various other tainted-product scares wiped milk, chicken, eggs and toothpaste from my shopping lists, and we got used to life without them.

I gave up dreaming about what would be in my American fridge back home: the cheeses, the olives, the mustards, the crackers. The steps needed to secure those things in China – the cross-town trips, the burdened traipsing home through crowds, and the inflated prices – were usually not worth it. One of our saddest days was when the authorities suddenly started planting cheese-sniffing beagles at the Beijing airport customs booths, making it absolutely clear that contraband cheese was a no-no to bring into the country. Our small circle of expats tracked the sniffer-dog sightings and sent around "cheese alert" emails to warn travelling friends heading back to China with cheese.

Instead, I learned to keep alert to opportunity that might come my way on the sidewalks where I walked along with the *lǎobǎixìng*. Occasionally, this strategy paid off.

Out on the small back streets, I might stumble upon a farmer from the countryside balancing baskets of fresh cherries over his shoulders, or a vendor and his 60-year-old tricycle cart piled high with heaps of terrific sports socks that looked like they fell off a Nike factory line in Guangdong. You never knew what you might run into. I was swept up in the enthusiasm of this *lǎobǎixìng* style of opportunistic behaviour. I always left our house with a few *rénmínbì*, an extra shopping bag and a sense of promise.

Occasionally, I made out like a bandit. One day, in a grocery store, I swept clean a shelf of microbrew beer for my husband and three giant jars of mustard, leaving none for future shoppers. It was victory tinged with guilt. What would the next expat shopper think, when looking for beer or mustard? I couldn't afford to think about them. Every man for himself, in modern China!

Another day, I looked in vain for a yoga mat, but instead tripped over dozens of frozen hind legs of pork, tossed onto the sidewalk in front of the sporting goods shop. Mountains of prosciutto, suddenly right there! This was so tempting; I imagined how excited my husband would be if I returned home with a giant prosciutto.

That was like one of those moments when you realise you are dreaming in a foreign language: I realised that I was thinking like a *lǎobǎixìng*. I was so close to securing that pork shank. But finally, I crept away, with the words "possibly dirty, very likely gone-bad prosciutto" nagging me.

If you took away the opportunistic part of shopping, the giant random fleamarket experience that is shopping in China, I wondered, what would be left? With no strings attached, what would lǎobǎixìng really want?

Answers to this question came from a variety of sources, via snippets from conversations, comments in books and newspapers, all confirmed by what I saw and heard myself. From a sociologist's tome:

In the 1950s and 1960s, the consumer items people sought ... *a watch, a bicycle, and a sewing machine.*

In the 1970s and 1980s they wanted ... *a colour television, a fridge, and a washing machine.*

By the late 1990s, they aspired to ... *take foreign holidays, purchase computers and cars, and to buy their own homes.*[11]

From a travel chronicler in 1988, as told by a market trader:

what people used to want were a bicycle, a radio, and a gas stove. Now, the Big Three are a refrigerator, a cassette machine and a color television.[12]

---

11 Gamble, Jos, *Shanghai in Transition*, Routledge, 2007.

12 Theroux, Paul, *Riding the Iron Rooster: By Train Through China*, Mariner, 2006.

At a conference I attended in Beijing in 2009, about the internet, censorship, technology and commerce, one exasperated Chinese participant finally blurted out that people, the *lǎobǎixìng*, aren't as preoccupied as Westerners about free speech and an uncensored internet: what *lǎobǎixìng* really want, he said, is … *a flush toilet, a refrigerator and a colour TV.*

This comment could have been taken straight from the Chinese government's stimulus spending package during the economic downturn of 2008–09, when it was offering a double-digit rebate to farmers for … refrigerators, colour TVs and mobile phones.

During one of the visits my husband and I made to rural Sichuan, this one a few months after the massively destructive earthquake of 2008, we accompanied American friends, who were anthropologists with more than fifteen years of fieldwork under their belts in the area.[13] We visited a village family, long known to our friends, who were building the house of their dreams.

Their dream was a far cry from the dream of Chinese farmers, before Mao's forced Communist collectivisation of the 1950s, when an old cliché held that the ideal rural life was "30 *mu* (two hectares) of land worked by an ox, plus many kids playing on *kang* (earthen bed heated in winter)."[14]

---

13 Thanks to John Flower and Pam Leonard.

14 http://www.btmbeijing.com/contents/en/btm/2009-01/feature/thegoodyearofox

The dream was bigger now. Too impatient to wait for its finish, the family were already living in their house, but short of windows or stair rails, and sleeping on mattresses tossed onto the floor. The shiny new toilet sat in the bathroom, free of any plumbing. Our friends who took us there came bearing the gift that was the family's fervent desire to own and immediately became the envy of the village: a new washing machine.

These are the *lǎobǎixìng*.

Nǐ hǎo, Wǒ jiào Mínyì
Hello, my name is Public Opinion

Chapter 6

A brief introduction to Chinese names

"THERE ARE TWO things you need to be considered a real person in China," our first contacts told us when we arrived in the country, "a mobile phone and a Chinese name."

So we fled from the sweltering steam bath of a Shanghai July day into the cool Raffles City shopping mall in search of the Nokia shop. Countless mall rats swarmed the escalators, thronged the open spaces, jockeyed for spots near a stage that had been set up for a live show. There were so many people and so much noise, although no one at all, I noticed, was inside any of the upmarket shops. The floors of Gucci, Prada, Diesel and Armani stood empty, a pattern we grew to expect in all the fancy malls around Shanghai.

Shanghai insiders outlined for us the chummy deal that explained the vacant stores: the stores paid rent as a percentage of their sales. So Shanghai, which could afford to underwrite the cheap rents, proudly touted the presence in their city of the classiest global brands. And the shops could add Shanghai to their bragging rights of operating in the world's classiest cities like New York, Tokyo, London, Hong Kong and Paris. Everyone had a reason to be happy.

The modest mobile phone shops, meanwhile, were busy with shoppers. Mobile phones are cheap in China, and service plans are cheaper. Migrant workers share phones and use them to keep in touch with their home towns and trade messages about the latest factory hirings and firings. Vendors whose tricycle carts are piled high with Styrofoam or plastic or cardboard can afford to own mobile phones. Young workers, students and taxi drivers have phones. People text more than they talk on the phones, because texting is even cheaper than talking. And reception is strong just about every- where: I have been in subway cars, on elevators, out in the countryside, and always with a perfect signal. Purchasing our phones was easy, and we plunged back into the Shanghai heat.

Getting a Chinese name was more difficult. A Chinese name was critical, our friends said; it would be our credibility, our bona fides. It would demonstrate that we weren't just here to flit around China, but intended to stick it out for a while. It would make it easier for those we met in China to think of us as "real" people.

Plus, the Chinese love names, although not necessarily difficult-to-pronounce foreign names.

My husband got quite excited about his name. I think he saw an opportunity for glamour. As an airplane buff, he had his eye on something that would capture the excitement of an ace fighter pilot. His Chinese friends played along. They tried, as is usual, to come up with a name that sounded in some way like his own name, and they also looked for a name that would somehow have an aura of strength, elegance and derring-do. The result, which they agreed met all the conditions, was Fāng Fēi Jié 方飞捷. The order of names in Chinese is normally the other way round from western names; the family name comes first, then middle, then first name.

Shanghai street sweeper on a texting break

Our last name, Fāng 方, is a popular family name in China, number 47 in the list of most-common surnames, to be exact. It is difficult to find a Chinese name that sounds close to Fallows, but at least Fang starts with more or less the same "fa" sound.

Fēi 飞 means "to fly". *Jié* 捷 can mean "triumph", or "victory", or "quick". Triumphant, quick flying. It may not be an ace fighter pilot, but it comes close. "Flyboy" perhaps? My husband loves his name, and he even bought a plaque for our family name Fāng 方, which he hung in our hall. Whenever Chinese people look at his business card, they cluck approvingly.

I was not so lucky with my name. My Chinese friends scratched their heads and sighed over every version of my first name, Deborah or Debbie or Deb. They parsed my name into two syllables: de + bi. They decided that "de" rhymes with *jiè* 借, pronounced like the first syllable of the word jeopardy. (My *jiè* 借 has the same sounds, but a different tone and different meaning from my husband's *jié* 捷.) My *jiè* means "to borrow" and it also means "to lend". The second sound, "bi", was easy. They chose *bǐ* 笔. It means "a pen", or "pencil", or "writing brush". The unfortunate result, however, was *jiè bǐ*, or "to borrow a pen". I could never quite get over the ridiculousness of my name whenever I greeted someone: "Hello, my name is 'to borrow a pen'." So, I more or less abandoned my Chinese name, and dodged along ingloriously for three years without one.

Even for the Chinese, assembling a Chinese name is quite a complicated job. I have a friend named Wáng Míng Yuán 王明元. Wáng, the family name, means "king". It is one of the most popular of all Chinese surnames; recent estimates say nearly one in every seven Chinese is named Wáng.

The middle name is traditionally used to keep order inside big families. Wáng Míng Yuán has many cousins, who all share the middle name Míng 明, which means "bright", to mark their generation. The need for middle names will become obsolete soon. With the one-child policy, which began in 1980, Wáng Míng Yuán's will be the last generation where it is normal to have siblings. Her children will have cousins, but her children's children probably won't.

Choosing a first name is a serious business. There are so many things to worry about: how does the name sound, along with the other names? Does it have an auspicious meaning, or does it at least sound like another auspicious word? What about the three names in a row, the family-middle-first names: do they together imply anything? How do the characters look, and how do they look together? Can a six-year-old learn to write them?

Yuán is my friend's first name. Yuán 元, as in "money". Money is a good and auspicious word. Yuán also sounds like *yuè* 月, which means "moon". That reminds one of her middle name, Míng, which is built from two characters together: 明, the sun 日 and the moon 月. It's no wonder that Chinese parents are given 30 days to name their children officially.

China has some odd-seeming traditions about first names. Chinese babies are often named impersonally, after timely events or milestones. During the year of China's first space launch, a lot of babies were named Wèixīng, meaning "satellite". After the earthquake of 2008, they were named Zhèn shēng, meaning "born during the earthquake". Before the Olympics, more than 3500 Chinese babies were named Aoyùn, meaning "Olympics".

During the Mao era, self-consciously loyal names were the rage: Yǒnghóng ("forever red"); Jiànguó ("build the country"); Aipíng ("love peace"); Jiànmín ("build the people"). More recently, serious policy-minded parents who followed the 11th National People's Congress named their children after some big issues: Shèbǎo or "social security", or Mínyì, which means "public opinion", and Héxié, which means "harmony".

Chinese can be very superstitious about names. One of my friends had a boyfriend when she was young, whose parents, according to a peasant custom, chose a powerful name intended to ward off *guǐ*, or evil spirits. His name was Fènduī, meaning "pile of shit".

The names of orphans are interesting. In the past they were processed with a blunt bureaucratic impersonality; children were often assigned a surname from the place where they were born. Children from Guǎngzhōu were named Guǎng; those from Shēnzhèn were named Shēn. Others were given "favourable" names like Hóng, meaning "red". Then some people worried about the disadvantage of being so easily identified and branded for life as an orphan. So orphanages began naming the babies Wáng, and Chén, some of China's most popular names, so the kids would blend in better.

Obvious problems arise when over a billion people share 100 family names. I still don't understand, for example, how it can possibly help to identify people by last name only, as newspapers always do. "A 35-year-old man, surname Wáng, was arrested for blackmailing his girlfriend … "

To help keep each other straight, the Chinese follow a few customs. Titles are important: Chén Lǎoshī, or Teacher Chén; Huáng Hùshi, or Nurse Huáng; Lǐ Yīshēng, or Doctor Lǐ; Zhāng Sījī, or Driver Zhāng; Zhōu Shīfu, or Master worker Zhōu, a respectful title for electricians and mechanics.

Nicknames help, too. Many of these are hold-overs from that first month before the parents could decide what to actually name their babies. Others, either cruel or affectionate, are picked up in primary school, like in every other country. Inside families, children are often just called big brother, (*gēge*) little sister (*mèimei*) and so on.

Most Chinese whom Westerners meet will also have an English name. This makes it easy on us, and the Chinese seem to like it, too. Hotels usually give English names to the housekeepers and doormen. Tour guides, upmarket shopkeepers and drivers have them, too. English teachers name their students, with varying results. Some are classic names like Catherine, Anna, Edward, Peter. Some are cute names, Kitty, Jacky, Sunny, Candy. Some are more interesting like Isaac, Kaiser, Hermes, Elvis, Felix. There are a few signs of English-teacher revenge: Winkie and Cutie.

A lot of young people told me they named themselves for characters in movies or books: Rocky cut my hair. He is from Guangdong, reputedly a hair-styling capital of China, although in truth, anytime I emerged from a hair salon not completely dissolved in tears, I considered that a good haircut. Rocky is a dreamer; he stands about 5'5" and weighs in at about 115 pounds. There are numerous Winnies (as in Pooh). And Emmas.

Many girls I knew named themselves for the sound of a word; one named Rain is a romantic kind of girl. Others because they like the thing it stands for; a girl named Apple likes apples.

Benjamin told me that multisyllable names are all the rage for guys now. His friends went online and came up with Christopher, Timothy and Nathaniel.

When foreigners become really popular in China, the Chinese will try to devise some rendition of their names that works –

Obama: *the US Embassy uses* ōu bā mǎ 欧巴马, *while the Chinese press renders it* ào bā mǎ 奥巴马.

Michael Phelps: fēi ěr pǔ sī 菲尔普斯 *works not so well.*

Bush: bù shí *and Reagan*: lǐ gēn *are OK.*
Shakespeare: shā shì bǐ yà *is not.*

Place names sound like so much mumbo-jumbo:

Los Angeles is luò shān jī.
New York is niǔ yuē.
Hollywood is hǎo lái wù.

At my tiny neighbourhood beauty shop in Beijing, a new girl appeared one day by the name of Xiǎo Xuē. Xiǎo rhymes with "meow", like a kitten's cry. And Xuē sounds like "shway". Lots of girls have Xiǎo, which means "little", as part of their name.

All the other girls in this shop had English names like Lily and Ruby. They all lived together, ate noodles together, gossiped about city boys, and went back to their home village during the New Year holidays to see their parents, who were generally not happy their daughters had fled for the big city. They told me that in their free time, they liked to go window-shopping. Most wore jeans and T-shirts from the cheap markets.

They spent their earnings on sequined sandals and high-heeled boots. They painted their own nails in shimmery colours, and when business was slow, they also painted flower designs on the faces of their mobile phones, which rang constantly with snippets of pop music. These girls were my channel to young Chinese cool.

Xiǎo Xuē was very awkward and shy at first. She tripped over the three-legged stools where the girls sat to do nails, necessitating any number of touch-ups. She refilled cups of hot water or tea for customers and stood against the wall, then later inched right up close to the customers to study and learn the trade. After a few weeks, the other girls decided Xiǎo Xuē was ready and assigned her to me. I am sure I was her first client. She was really, really slow.

When I asked Xiǎo Xuē if she had an English name like the other girls, she shot me a silent look – reminding me instantly that she was fresh from Shanxi, a poor, dismal, coal-mining province – that said: "How in the world would I have got an English name?" When I asked her if she would like to have one, she nodded yes right away.

I considered names that sounded kind of like her own: Sharon, Sandy, Sasha. Xiǎo Xuē listened and without hesitating even a second, said Sasha. That is how Xiǎo Xuē became my responsibility and how I gave her the name she might use for the rest of her working life.

Xiǎo Xuē now had one foot in the traditional old China where she was born, and Sasha had the other foot in the new, global world whose reach includes even a small beauty shop in Beijing.

东北

Dōngběi Eastnorth

Chapter 7

Finding your way in China – the semantics of time and place

FROM OUR 22ND-FLOOR apartment in Shanghai, I could peer down at the troupes of early risers practising tai chi in the park. I studied them with my binoculars each morning for several weeks, searching for a small group that looked like they might be sympathetic to my stepping in alongside them.

I spied one possibility: a cluster of about ten men and women who, like most who practise tai chi, looked to be in their seventies and who somehow struck me as accepting. This was their daily ritual: one thin man, clearly their leader, rode up on his Flying Pigeon bicycle. He took his old-fashioned tape player from the bike basket and placed it on the low wall of the small esplanade. The others slowly gathered around chatting for a few moments. Then the thin man took out his tape, put it in the machine and clicked play. On that signal, everyone claimed a spot and the practice began.

One morning as the sun rose, I drew moral support from a friend visiting from New York, and together we gingerly approached them. They figured out our intentions right away. A very tiny woman beckoned us over with a little downward wave of her palm, and that was the beginning of my long relationship. I realised my only mistake had been waiting so long to make an approach. For the next five months, until hard winter set in, my new friends tucked me into their ranks, making sure I was always in eyeshot of someone to follow, and they gently bossed me around, all in the name of improvement.

Our tai chi corner of the park was not a street but served as a thoroughfare of sorts for morning commuters. Bicycles regularly threaded through our lines, often between our "high pat the horse" move and "kick to the left". An occasional motor scooter did the same, its driver revving the limp little motor and leaning on the piercing horn. A certain salaryman in his dark blue pants and white shirt, carrying his worn briefcase, marched through our ranks every day as he headed for work. He walked facing backwards, and at a brisk pace. No one batted an eye at his backwards gait, as though it was the most natural thing in the world. I hid my astonishment, both at him and at the absence of interest from anyone else in my group.

Early-morning tai chi in Shanghai's People's Park

For me, this was the moment I started to realise there is a gap between my western perspective toward the physical world – order, place, direction, and even time – and that of the Chinese.

Take reading and writing, for example. If you ask a Westerner about reading, you're likely to get a rigid sense of direction and order: left to right, top row to bottom, just like you are reading right now. Chinese orientation is less predictable. Traditionally, Chinese was read in vertical columns, from top to bottom, and from right to left.

Familiarity with western languages and modern tech- nologies changed that, and the Chinese now generally read like we do. Chinese newspapers switched from vertical columns to horizontal rows in the mid-1950s.

Sometimes shape still dictates direction: Chinese characters on vertical banners are written top to bottom. Inscriptions over old temple gates are read right to left. Oddly, some tour buses have text written from the front to the rear along each side of the bus, that is from right to left on the right side of the bus and from left to right on the left side. Business cards are written however the owner designs them.

There is more. Our western presentation of a word is as a group of letters bound together and marked off from other words by the physical space around them. But Chinese words written in characters are not bound by space. Each character, even if it is half of a two-character word, is separated equally from its neighbour. There is no telling where a word begins and ends – itwouldbeasifyouwere-readingthetextthisway.

The tradition of classical Chinese went a step further back: there was not even punctuation to mark sentences. Today, when the Chinese write out English translations, close enough is often good enough: the local fast-food shop in our Beijing neighbourhood was called "Bee Fnoodles".

Beyond text, the Chinese sense of position and place out in the real world differs from ours, too. There are a number of quaint tidbits, all reflected in the language. For example, my language teachers all taught us to think of Chinese as moving the focus from big to small: addresses telescope in from country, to city, to street, to number, to apartment. Personal names are ordered to start big with the family name and end small with the personal name. Dates are referenced from year to month to day.

Or, when it comes to finding your bearings in China, east-west is the predominant axis, not our familiar north-south. You start with the east or west: in Shanghai, we lived near the westnorth, or *xībĕi* section of People's Park. We would sometimes fly on Northwest Airlines, or Xībĕi, Westnorth in Chinese. Southeast Asia is Dōngnán, or Eastsouth Asia in Chinese. Manchuria is Dōngbĕi, or Eastnorth in China.

This concept is easy to grasp, but putting it into practice is harder than you'd guess. Even after years, this pattern does not come naturally to me. In Beijing, we lived at the intersection of two major roads. I directed taxis so often to the *dōngnán jiǎo*, or eastsouth corner of our intersec-tion, that it rolled off my tongue. But, in almost any other circumstance, I was like a primary school kid counting up sums on my fingers: I had to calculate my bearings step by step, first the actual geography, then the English words, then the reverse translation.

Beyond linguistic eccentricities, I find the ultimately curious – and confusing – reference point in the Chinese sense of world order is the conflation of two concepts, place and time, into a pair of antonyms: *xià* and *shàng*.

In Mandarin, *shàng* 上 is a common word whose meaning extends to a lot of different words in English: "up", "on top", "above", "on". *Xià* 下 is its antonym, the word for "down", "under", "below", "beneath", "off".

Shànghǎi = *above the sea*
Wǒ shàng lóu = *I go upstairs*
Lóu shàng = *upstairs*
Zài lù shàng = *on the street*
Shàng fēijī = *get on the plane*
Shān shàng = *on the top of the mountain*

Xiàmén (a pretty coastal city south of Shanghai) = below + gate = *below the gate*
Wǒ xià lóu = *I go downstairs*
Lóu xià = *downstairs*
Zài zhuōzi xià = *under the table*
Xià chē = *get off the train (car)*
Shān xià = *at the foot of the mountain*

Simple enough. But Chinese also uses the same pair of words, *xià* and *shàng*, to refer to time. *Shàng* 上 refers to the past, as in last or previous; *xià* 下 refers to the future, as in next.

Shàng Xīngqī èr = *last Tuesday*
Shàng ge yuè = *last month*

Xià ge yuè = *next month*
Xià cì = *next time*

My language teacher introduced both these concepts of place and time in the same lesson. Maybe it made sense to her that we should just cover all the meanings of *shàng* and *xià* at once, but it was hopelessly confusing to us.

To sort it out, I tried drawing diagrams with arrows of *shàng* pointing up for place and back for time, with *xià* pointing down for direction and forward for time. Other struggling fellow students invented their own clues to remember this (to us) arbitrary system. Our teacher seemed surprised that we had so much trouble, baffled that we didn't find it normal that place and time were melded into a single word, which was the way her world worked.

On my daily forays, I ran into many practical examples of geographic dissonance with China. Deep in the bowels of the subway systems, I often joined a small crowd of riders – foreigners, but often Chinese too – gathered around the station maps, studying to get our bearings on the world above ground and to choose the best exit. We scratched our collective heads in confusion over the maps. Sometimes south is at the top of the map, sometimes north. Sometimes there are two maps side by side, but oriented upside down from each other. Occasionally, there is a third kind of map, drawn from the real-time perspective of the person viewing it, like the diagrams tacked to the inside of hotel room doors that direct you to the nearest exit.

The maps I consider upside down are no accident or mistake by Chinese standards. The proud litany of "The Four Great Inventions of China" includes the compass, along with paper, printing and gunpowder. Here is the orientation of an early Chinese compass:

There were good reasons for this compass orientation, at least in early times: south was auspicious, being the source of comforting warm breezes and the best sunshine. North was feared for the biting, brittle winds and invading barbarians. Beijing's Forbidden City was designed to be mindful of this *fēngshuǐ* – literally "wind-water" sense. The main gates of the Forbidden City open to the sunny south, and the back walls guard against the angry, invading Mongols to the north.

The Forbidden City was the scene of my one and only experience as a time-traveller. I was visiting

Beijing briefly during the spring of 2003, just as China was emerging from its lockdown during the SARS epidemic. Schools had been closed and businesses quieted. It was later determined that this marked the moment when Chinese youth became hooked on video games, as kids spent long days at home with little else to do. Street-cleaning trucks sprayed disinfectant along all the kerbs with manic ferocity; the subways were just starting up again and still eerily, blessedly empty; and a few tourist spots were opening their gates.

I went one day to the Forbidden City, the lone visitor in all the courtyards and alleyways. With every step, I heard only my own sandals clacking against the stones and the wind through the trees in the back gardens. I sat in the gardens studying my maps and discovered that sure enough, in the vestige of the original city plan, the top of the city, at the top of the map, was south, while the so-called "right" gate of the city was in the direction of west.

Maps have been my lifeline as I have travelled around China. I have collected maps to help navigate all the big, sprawling cities – Shenzhen, Shenyang, Chengdu, Urumqi, Hangzhou, Nanjing, Kunming; the list goes on.

My collection has grown into towering stacks, and I hoard them as protectively as a pensioner who harbours stray cats. My maps are invaluable, but they are also problematic, drawn with little consistency and less reliability, like those in the subway stations.

Each time I head out to a first-time destination even in my home cities of Shanghai and Beijing, I follow a sacred ritual of preparation. I choose my best three or four maps for the city, spread them out on the dining-room table, and cross-check against a variety of web sources. This isn't obsession; it is survival. After three years in China, my success rate for first-time direct hits reached about 60%.

In fairness, Chinese map-makers face a big task just keeping pace with change. Within weeks, roads disappear or appear, names change, buildings pop up where others have been razed. In Shanghai, I learned to wait patiently beside the cobbler repairing my shoes or risk them vanishing overnight along with the shop, sacrifices to progress. I developed a keen sensitivity about shops that looked like they could have short lifespans and was always diligent about collecting left laundry promptly. One of my most disappointing losses was several coupons on my prepaid discount card at the local massage parlour. I returned after Chinese New Year holidays one year to find its doors shuttered and a few abandoned, sorry-looking beds. No note, no map, nothing.

When my maps fail me, I ask people on the street for help. The dialogue always goes something like this:

Me: Bówùguǎn zài nǎr? ("*Can you tell me where the museum is?*")

Good-natured Chinese pedestrian: Zài nàr! (*"Over there"* – this accompanied by a broad sweep, arcing 90 degrees or more, of two widespread arms, and ending with a delicate upward flair of the wrist, all of which points toward nothing in particular).
Me: Xìe xie. (*"Thanks,"* while thinking, I haven't a clue where this person is gesturing me to go; shall I go straight ahead, or shall I cross to the right?)
Good-natured Chinese pedestrian: Silence (with a look that says, *"Another crazy foreigner, asking for directions and then disregarding them"*).

What is it about this dysfunctional business of maps and directions? One long-time China hand told me he thinks the vagueness is connected to the deep-seated sense of face: the Chinese find it very personally difficult to say boldly and simply "I don't know" when they don't know an answer. They are more comfortable – and can save face – by demurring and offering some vague noncommittal response. This explanation made sense to me, although I would have much preferred to hear a straightforward "I don't know" than be sent off frequently on a wild-goose chase.

Another explanation came from a young Chinese woman named Miranda, who described the problem in terms of practical, functional training and experience.

Miranda works in an English-speaking office and uses a giant exercise ball as her desk chair. She drifted onto my wavelength easily and was always patient about answering my questions.

This time, she was surprised by my map-reading query, "Why don't the Chinese use maps?" And I was surprised by her answer. "Map-reading," Miranda almost scoffed, "Why would you need it? If you live in a village you know where you're going. We don't study map-reading in school."

"Now," she continued, "if you're in the army, then you study maps. But if you're not in the army, you don't need them."

Mostly fair enough, I thought (although you would think that taxi drivers, who always make calls on their cell phones but never turn to maps when they need directions, might be an exception), but what if you're off in another part of the country besides your home village? Miranda agreed that the Chinese did seem to have trouble finding their way around in new places. She said, "If you ask someone where their home town is, they'll say it is seven hours by bus. Or four hours by train. They won't tell you *where* it is."

Hearing a question of *where* and giving an answer of *how long*; walking *backwards* to get somewhere *in front of* you; reading maps *upside down*; absorbing that *up in space* also means *behind in time* and *down in space* also means *ahead in time*: these are some of the points where East meets West.

Wǒ, Nǐ, Tā, Tā, Tā   I, You, He, She, It

Chapter 8

Disappearing pronouns and the sense of self

THE VILLAGE OF Xizhou is nestled in a verdant strip of land in China's southwestern Yunnan Province. To the east lies Erhai Lake, where cormorants play. To the west, hills rise to the Tibetan Plateau, where herders graze their yaks. During World War II, Xizhou offered a first contact point for the Flying Tigers as they flew over the "Hump" of the Himalayas, laden with supplies for Chiang Kai-shek's army in Chungking (now Chongqing, by some measures China's most populous metropolitan area). The American military set up a radar and radio station for the fliers in the attic room of a Xizhou village elder's farmhouse.

That farmer's son still lives in the same small house. His dog yapped when he heard us knocking at the gate, and his daughter invited us to look around, and later for tea. There were few signs of events in what we considered the historic past, but the old man, who witnessed the excitement as a little boy, conjured up images for us of soldiers pacing and smoking in the yard, and parking their shiny automobiles behind the outbuildings where empty fields now stand. We looked around the attic and peeked into some old storage barrels, hoping to find a cast-off bit of hardware or a little writing scratched on the wall somewhere. But there was nothing, not a remnant left.

Xizhou, which means something like "happy land", is blessed with many gifts of nature – rice paddies, elegant hills, a temperate climate and the clearest skies we saw in all our years in China. Xizhou saved itself by its own charms during the Cultural Revolution. Troops from the People's Liberation Army decided to quarter there. Their presence protected the buildings from the predations of the Red Guards, who roamed the country and wreaked havoc with abandon. Townspeople buried their treasures and heirlooms for safekeeping in the fields around their houses; now they will sell some of what they have unearthed to visitors and tourists. I bought a small teapot and a few mirrors from someone's attic.

The town looks prosperous compared with many we saw in China. Farmers are busy in their lush paddies. The forward-minded town authorities are helping restore old houses. Xizhou kids ride bikes and wear nice shoes. When school was letting out one afternoon, we saw three or four kids pause their bikes at the snack shop by the main square, furtively buy two cans of the weak local beer, zip them quickly into their backpacks and ride off.

On Saturday evenings in Xizhou, there is an "English-corner" for informal conversation, in one of the village play yards. It was started by some American friends of ours, who opened a small cultural centre and inn in the village. About a dozen kids showed up the evening we were there, to play games and practise their English with any English speakers who might show up. A few curious parents hovered around the edges of the group, and a few more sat in the circle among the children to absorb what they could.

In between singing and dancing the hokey-cokey and some other favourites we dredged up from our own school days, we enticed the kids with a circle game into a bit of an English pronoun lesson. Each one had to tell the age of the kid sitting next to him: "This is Ming. She is twelve years old." Or "This is Liang. He is eleven years old." The kids caught on right away, but when one would confuse "he" and "she", the rest, like vultures, would home in screaming mercilessly "HE! HE!!" or "SHE! SHE!!"

Mixing up he and she in English is a classic error among the Chinese. I came to expect that even the most fluent Chinese speakers of English would eventually say something like "Your son looks just like your husband; she is tall and handsome!"

This confusion never occurs on formal occasions, like speeches or presentations. I never see it in print. But the he/she mix-ups regularly show up in everyday conversation. "Oh yeah, my wife does that," two different Americans with very fluent English-speaking Chinese spouses told me. A Chinese woman who spent time abroad and speaks with an easy American accent told me, "I hear myself talking and the wrong word just pops out before I know it!"

What is going on here? The simplest answer – that "he" and "she" are both said as *tā* in Chinese – is tempting, but it is not enough. The concept of gender is simple, and the Chinese commonly master much worse sticklers in English, like verb tenses. Certainly they could master this, especially considering *tā* "he" and *tā* "she" are represented in their written forms by two different characters: *tā* "he" is 他 and "she" is 她.

I was chatting about *tā* and the characters for writing it with a calligrapher in Xizhou one day. (Chinese chat about things like this!) He told me that the character for "she" 她, is a new arrival, created not even 100 years ago, in the 1920s, during one of the many periods when the Chinese were debating about their writing systems. Should they simplify some characters? (Mao did this later.) Should they use a phonetic writing system? (There have been several; Pinyin is now taught in schools.) Should they create a new character for "she" to distinguish it from "he"? Arguments raged, and eventually the character 她 was accepted, although a brief flirtation with introducing a new way of pronouncing 她 as *yī* got no traction. The new character for "she"/ *tā* would seem logical to Chinese speakers, since the left-hand part of the character 女 is the character for "woman".

A further explanation about the confusions with *tā* is that the Chinese aren't as smitten with using pronouns at all, including *tā*, as are speakers of most western languages. Pronouns just aren't that important to the Chinese, and they omit them frequently. A good rule of thumb for Chinese would be: unless you really need to use the pronoun to clarify the context, or highlight the antecedent of the pronouns, or otherwise draw attention in some way, just leave it out. From the Chinese point of view, I suppose they might say that the rest of the world litters its speech with unnecessary pronouns.

An example in one of my grammar books illustrates how frequently "I" and all the other pronouns can easily be omitted in Chinese. Try to read the following (translated) passage without saying any of the words that appear in parentheses:

That day I went to see an old friend. (I) knocked on the door (but) nobody answered. (I) thought that he must have gone out, (and) so (I) left a note (and) pushed (it) through the letter box in the door indicating that (I) would come back another day.

(I) also said that as soon as (he) comes back, it would be nice if (he) could drop me a note. (I) never expected that a few days later (I) would receive an anonymous letter saying that he had already moved out ... [15]

During my early days of trying to speak Chinese, when I still fell back on word-for-word translations from English, I grew to be self-conscious about saying *wǒ, wǒ, wǒ* (I, I, I) all the time. "I'm afraid I'm late." "I'm hungry." "I'm terribly lost." I knew this wasn't quite right, but it felt vague and unresolved to simply say, "Late" or "Hungry" or "Terribly lost".

But if I was guilty of using far too many pronouns in Chinese, I would argue back that the Chinese go way too soft on their pronoun use in English, particularly their lack of attention to he and she. Some English-speaking Chinese offered their own explanations of what was going on with he and she, explanations ranging from China's educational system to children's cognitive development to the Mandarin sound system.

The Chinese education system excels in teaching to tests, particularly to the *gāokǎo*, China's uniquely important college entrance exam. "The tests," an American English teacher in China writes, "focus on

---

15 Yip, Po-Ching and Rimmington, Don, *Chinese: A Comprehensive Grammar*, Routledge, 2003.

recognising esoteric vocabulary and grammar rather than being able to use the basics in flexible and expressive ways."[16] By this prescription, colloquial use of he and she falls through the cracks; it's not going to come up in the exam. So while my Chinese teachers could talk me under the table about the most arcane grammatical concepts in English or Chinese, even they faltered on he and she in conversation.

The teachers just don't drill pronouns, one Chinese friend told me, and getting no practice means you are always performing "an alien mental calculation" to come up with a choice of he or she. "Alien mental calculation," I scoffed to myself, reflecting on my struggles with word order in Mandarin sentences, which (at least to my mind) requires a much more complicated formula to master than a simple choice between he and she. But to be perfectly fair, I would concede that the choice of he or she is made harder for the Chinese to master by all the variants of him/her, his/hers, and his/her in English. All these are reduced to *tā* in Chinese.

One of my most reliable language resources, Miranda, a young Chinese woman, said she thought that the source of vagueness occurred well before going to school. It's all about cognition and development, she ventured. English speakers have to run into the concept

---

16 http://jamesfallows.theatlantic.com/archives/2009/05/todays_chapter_on_chinese_educ.php#more

of pronoun gender in language from the word go, because they have to distinguish he and she. But for the Chinese, it isn't an important concept. Cognitively, everything is *tā*. Only later, once children begin to read and write the characters 他 and 她 are they even introduced to the concept of gender in language.

This explanation makes for a kind of reality check on what we consider the givens of language. We think the distinction between he and she is so important, but wait – the Chinese can do very well without it, thank you very much! This "given" is actually a reflection of the structure of English, just as the "givens" of gender assigned to every French noun (*la maison* (f.), *le travail* (m.) are a reflection of the structure of French.

Jessie, a Chinese woman who spent a year at university in New York recently, said the Chinese sound system is to blame for the problems of keeping he and she straight. "He and she sound a lot the same to Chinese speakers. It's easy to get mixed up," she said. Much like our trouble with tones, I thought. Many Chinese just don't *hear* the difference.

In English, the "h" and "sh" sounds, as in "he" and "she", are produced very differently. The tongue is in different positions, and the air passes around the tongue in different ways. So, to English speakers, "he" and "she" are easily distinguishable words; no native speaker would confuse the two. It's not the same for Chinese speakers. The sound system of their language does not include either "he" or "she" as we pronounce them in English. These are not sounds that Chinese speakers recognise easily or know how to say. Instead they know the syllable *xi* – which English speakers don't recognise or find easy to say, and which sounds to us like a blend of "he" and "she", or else like "see". So, apart from other reasons for forgetting whether "he" or "she" is correct in a given sentence, Chinese speakers may sometimes say "she" when meaning "he", since it is so hard for them to hear the difference.

Back home in smoggy Beijing, I was thinking about English-corner in Xizhou and wondering if the pronoun lesson would stick with any of the kids. Perhaps there would be a clutch of Chinese kids who would grow up using he and she flawlessly. But probably not; if even my Chinese teachers don't use them correctly, the odds are stacked against the kids from Xizhou.

I was also thinking about an experience with the "I" pronoun that really caught my ear during one of my early lessons at the Miracle Mandarin language school in Shanghai. Our teacher used to have us students give little impromptu presentations whenever class became too dull. That certainly woke us up. The topics were normally the mundane "What I did over the weekend" variety. But one day, she asked us to talk about "What I believe in". All of us students started with the predictable western concepts of democracy, or free speech or pursuit of happiness. It was hard, especially given our limited vocabulary in Mandarin.

When my turn came, I stalled for time by asking our teacher, Sandy, to tell us what she believed in. Sandy, who was very earnest and a diligent teacher, paused for a moment, and then declared almost defiantly: "*I BELIEVE IN MYSELF.*"

We were stunned. Sandy was normally shy, still learning to stand her ground in front of a class of brash Westerners, and typically did not assert her personality into the business of her teaching. Her defiance was remarkable to me in two ways: one for what she said (the outright declaration) and one for how she said it (her use of pronouns). And they were connected. Sandy recognised and was declaring that, once raised and educated, her destiny was singularly up to her. She could well have been speaking for the whole cohort of people in their twenties, who are growing up in a very different China from that of their parents. Sandy's generation will not see the cradle-to-grave care and control that the state both provided for and imposed on earlier generations. This was a new world, where she would make her own way.

And when Sandy said, "*I* believe in *myself*", there was nothing wishy-washy about how she said it. She knew precisely that using those pronouns beamed the attention right on herself. I wondered if she also knew how this use of "self" flew in the face of the tone of her parents' generation, who grew up during the Cultural Revolution.

From a novel by a Chinese woman who relocated to London:

> *We Chinese are not encouraged to use the word "self" so often. The old comrades in the work unit would say, how can you think of "self" most of the time but not about others and the whole society?*[17]

What I never learned was why Sandy made her declaration in English. This was our Chinese class, after all, and we would have understood her Chinese at that point: *Wǒ xiāngxìn wǒ zìjǐ* 我相信我自己 "I believe I self." Did speaking English somehow free Sandy up to go straight for the pronouns and ram her point home? I don't know the answer to that, but I do know that we were impressed.

---

17 Guo, Xiaolu, *A Concise Chinese-English Dictionary for Lovers,* Doubleday, 2007, p. 213.

热闹

Rènao   Hot-and-noisy

Chapter 9

Think like the Chinese think

WALKING HOME ONE drizzly night along Shanghai's busy Nanjing Lu, I passed a labourer doing road-work. He was submerged to his ankles in a soggy trench, wearing rubber flip-flops and wielding a heavy, sparking blowtorch. It looked very dangerous. Most mornings as I walked to school along the same road, I watched restaurant staff hosing down their concrete deck. They padded around puddles in their bare feet, plugging and unplugging radios, fans and electric tools.

There is more: one day I passed a telephone linesman who hooked his homemade ladder over a set of swinging cables, then clambered up and edged like a tightrope walker along the tension wires fifteen feet above the ground. In Shanghai pairs of window cleaners routinely dangle and sway tens of stories high, buckets and squeegies in hand, secured only to each other at opposite ends of a rope that hooks around some invisible rooftop anchor. One day in Beijing, I watched half a dozen workers struggling to right a toppled and leaking gasoline can atop their rickety cart, puffing all the while on their cigarettes. Daily, I wanted to cry out "*Xiǎoxīn!*" Look out, Be careful, Watch out!

China can be a dangerous place. The papers are filled with reports of mining disasters, bus crashes and construction site collapses. An average of 250 people die every day from accidents of all sorts. A fire in an upper stairwell of Shanghai's World Financial Center, until recently the tallest building in the world, slowed down work for a while in the summer of 2007. During the 2008 Sichuan earthquake, thousands of the so-called "tofu-dregs schoolhouses" 豆腐渣校舍 collapsed from shoddy construction.

In Shanghai, taxi drivers routinely work 24-hour shifts. In that city I can count three separate terrifying taxi rides, where I sat peering from the back seat at the rear-view mirror, watching the driver's eyelids droop as the car started to weave. Desperate to keep the driver awake, my husband and I would engage in loud faux-arguments, or shamelessly poke and prod the driver to rouse him (or, in one case, her) into consciousness.

Xiǎoxīn! (shyao sheen) means "Watch out!" *Xiǎo – xīn* is literally "small – heart". I envision my own heart closing tightly, becoming very small, when I see these dangerous acts. Sometimes *xiǎoxīn* is used as an adjective that means "cautious" or "careful", as in "He is a naturally cautious driver". Sometimes mothers cry out "*Xiǎoxīn!*" to their children approaching crossings.

My language books tell me that in China "ancient people believed that the heart – *xīn* – was related to thinking and temperament", in sentiments like desire, fear, love and respect. Hence, *xīn* finds its way into many feeling-related compound words:

Kāixīn = kāi *(open)* + *heart* = *joyous*
Fàngxīn = fàng *(put in place)* + *heart* = *set your mind at ease*
Shāngxīn = shāng *(wound)* + *heart* = *heart-broken*
Rèxīn = rè *(hot)* + *heart* = *enthusiastic or warmhearted*

Coining compound words, like *kāixīn* (joyous) or *xiǎoxīn* (danger) is one way to give names to new concepts or ideas, inventions, or nuances of sophistication. If simple words cover the basics of civilisation – words like hot, cold, sun, moon, food, tree, mother, hand, walk and die – then compound words step up to the next stage with words like whirlpool, snowman, brainstorm, sunglasses, skyline, tiptoe, heartbroken. Chinese has been adding compounds to its lexicon for hundreds, even thousands of years. In Old Chinese, about 20% of words were compounds; in modern Chinese, about 80%.

English has lots of compound words, too, although not nearly as many as Chinese. English speakers took a different tack to expand their lexicon and largely added new words by outright borrowing of words from other languages. Thanks largely to the invading Normans in 1066, nearly half the vocabulary of modern English is borrowed from French. There are so many words – words like admire, comic, foliage, imbecile, mountain, simple ... Borrowed words provide great clues for tracking how, when and where people bumped into (or pillaged and plundered) each other and influenced (or dominated and subjugated) each other when roaming around the early world. People moved around the earth, leaving their words behind for others, or picking up new ones.

Chinese has just a meagre collection of borrowed words. And because of the limited syllable structure in Chinese, it is difficult to "sinify" the words from other languages. So, the small lexicon of Chinese borrowed words bears little resemblance to their origins: *mòtè*, (model, as in fashion model), *qiǎokèlì* (chocolate), *shālā* (salad), *luómàn* (romance) and *luóji* (logic).

Borrowed words may provide windows into historical population migrations and movements, but compound words open windows into a people's own evolving culture. Compounds are very homegrown in nature; as we saw above, *xīn*, the heart, was so important to Chinese culture that it became the lynchpin of many different ideas and sensibilities.

One way Chinese makes a lot of compound words is to glue together two antonyms, or opposites, into a new whole. This fits right in comfortably with the concept of *yīn yáng*, which still permeates Chinese philosophy, medicine, nature, martial arts and nutrition even today. In *yīn yáng*, two opposing forces connect or meld into each other and make up a greater whole. On one side, the *yīn* is feminine, moon, dark, cold, passive, shady. On the other, the *yáng* is masculine, sun, bright, hot, active, clear (don't blame me!). The aim is to achieve a blend and balance of the two forces.

阴 阳
yīn yáng

Some other examples are:

Kāiguān is kāi *(open)* + guān *(close), a switch, as in to switch on and off a light. "Will you open-close the light?"*

Hǎohuài is hǎo *(good)* + huài *(bad), meaning quality. "The good-bad of this cloth makes it look cheap."*

Duōshǎo *is* duō *(many, much)* + shǎo *(few, little),*
meaning how many or how much. "Do you have
much-little time to spend with me?"

Hūxī *is* hū *(exhale)* + xī *(inhale)* = *breathe. "Exhale-*
inhale polluted air is bad for you."

Zuǒyòu *is* zuǒ *(left)* + yòu *(right)* = *approximately,*
nearly or about. "There is enough coffee to make
left-right one more pot."

Dōngxi *is* dōng *(east)* + xi *(west)* = *stuff or things.*
"I'm going out to get a few east-west for the
house."

Gāoǎi *is* gāo *(tall)* + ǎi *(short)* = *height. "I started*
to notice the number of newspaper ads for jobs that
came with prerequisites for a candidate's minimum
tall-short."

Dàxiǎo *is* dà *(big)* + xiǎo *(small)* = *size. "Which*
big-small do you want to try on?"

Chinese makes compounds in many ways besides
slapping together opposites. In the era of technology,
Chinese seized the word *diàn*, 电, which means power,
electricity or electronics, and tacked other existing
words onto it as names for new electric and digital

inventions.[18] Patterns like this can be a godsend to language students trying to build their vocabulary.

Diànhuà = *electricity* + huà *(speech)* = *telephone or telephone call*

Diànnǎo = *electric* + nǎo *(brain) meaning computer*

Diànshì = *electric* + shì *(view) = TV*

Diàntī = *electric* + tī *(stairs) = elevator, lift*

Diànyǐng = *electric* + yǐng *(shadow) = movie or film*

Diànbào = *electric* + bào *(report) = telegram or cable*

Diànchē = *electricity* + chē *(vehicle) = tram or streetcar*

Many Chinese compounds are straightforward literal translations of their parts, while others are so vivid that they easily make sense:

---

18 In this case, Chinese had borrowed a lot of *diàn* words from Japanese. Japan modernised earlier, and they created new compound words for technological terms and western ideas based on their own characters, some of which Chinese later adopted.

Fùmǔ = fù *(father)* + mǔ *(mother)* = *parent*

Yǔmào = yǔ *(rain)* + mào *(hat)* = *rainhat*

Míngbai = míng *(clear)* + bai *(white)* = *understand*

Yānhóng = yān *(eye)* + hóng *(red)* = *jealous*

Niánqīng = nián *(year, age)* + qīng *(light)* = *young*

Tiānqì = tiān *(heaven)* + qì *(breath)* = *weather*

Huǒchē = huǒ *(fire)* + chē *(car, wagon)* = *train*

Other compounds come from idioms, but are so far removed from current use or even forgotten, that there is no connecting them to the literal meaning of their parts.

Mǎmahūhū= mǎ (horse) + *hū* (tiger) = horse-horsetiger-tiger or "so so", as in "How are things going at work? Well, *mǎmahūhū*." I heard a fable about the origin of this word. I usually shun folk etymologies for their lack of linguistic rigour and accountability, but this one is particularly charming: an artist was drawing an animal picture on the wall of his cave. His neighbours came along, saw the work, were impressed and began arguing over whether the animal was a horse or a tiger. The arguments escalated until the village folk stepped back, got a grip and realised that if they could not agree on what the drawing represented, then perhaps it wasn't actually so good after all. Hence, horsehorsetigertiger, or *mǎmahūhū*, became the shortcut way to describe the quality of something as so-so.

Mǎshàng = *mǎ* (horse) + *shàng* (on, above), on the horse meaning "immediately" or "right away". "I'm coming right away." A good guess would be that *mǎshàng* got its meaning way back when the fastest way to get somewhere was on a horse.

There are some compound words that go right to the heart of Chinese life. One is *rènao, rè* (hot) + *nào* (noisy).[19]

My dictionary defines *rènao* 热闹 as "noisy and exciting in a pleasant way, boisterous, bustling". This odd definition doesn't do justice to the real-world connotations of the word. *Rènao* is all about the revelry of a festive, chaotic gathering. Think of a raucous, beery sports bar during the Superbowl, or a loud, sweaty pub during the World Cup. *Rènao* is the default mode of Chinese social life; it is the standard to strive for.

At a *rènao* restaurant in China, diners squeeze around too-small tables that are squeezed into too-small spaces. They toast, drink, tell stories, pass food, hop from their seats to drink to each other, sing, laugh, eat.

---

19 The fourth tone on *nào* is lost when it becomes part of the compound word *rènao*.

Servers bustle from table to table, bringing more and more dishes, opening more and more bottles. Diners call after servers, servers run faster. The measure of a great evening is the hotter and noisier the better.

A good train ride is also *rènao*. My first ride was from Shanghai to Hangzhou; people jumbled together with their snacks, papers, children, thermoses of hot tea, ringing mobile phones, bags of belongings, all amidst loudspeakers, pushcarts of food, and dashing up and down the aisles. It was a whole village life recreated inside one car of the train. On overnight rides, people change into sleeping clothes, trail back and forth to the bathroom, play cards, tell stories, make new friends.

If foreigners are exhausted by *rènao*, Chinese are energised by it.

Then there is *xìngfú*: *xìng* (good fortune) + *fú* (happiness) = happy, fortunate. The first and only time I heard the word was in a conversation with Sasha, the young girl from Shanxi Province, who worked in a beauty shop near where we lived.

Four-dollar manicures proved to be an irresistible respite for me from the otherwise chaotic pace of our China life. When we first moved to Shanghai, a young local woman was assembling a list for me of places for cheap but clean foot massages, mani-pedis, facials and haircuts, the affordable stuff of even working girls in China. Suddenly she stopped as if surprised at herself and blurted out: "Shanghai is a great city for girls!"

If these luxuries need justifying, it's easy to talk yourself into the idea that they also provide a great chance to practise language skills. Sasha was telling me about her visit home over the previous holidays, and asking me about plans to go back to America. I told her *xiàtiān*, summer, which was then about two months away. She asked when I would be returning, and I replied that it would be a long while, since we were moving back home after three years in China. "I will be happy to be nearer to our children, and all of our family," I said.

Sasha paused for just a second longer than usual, and said "*Xìngfú*." I wasn't sure I understood her at the time, and gave a kind of nod and half-smile, the way you do when trying to cover for your shortcomings in a foreign language. At least I knew that both *xìng* and *fú* had a positive sense, so this must be a good word.

Once home, I looked up *xìngfú* in my dictionary, which elaborated on the standard definition of "fortunate". *Xìngfú*, it said, is "used in a sublime sense, denoting a profound and almost perfect happiness".

That was a poignant moment for me. Sasha, a working girl from the coal provinces of the middle of China, had plucked out a perfect word to describe our homegoing to our family and friends.

I try now to appreciate the compound words, in English as well as in Chinese. I try to not let them become so commonplace that I don't really hear what lies behind them.

听不懂

Tīng bù dǒng I don't understand

Chapter 10

A billion people; countless dialects

MY WORST EXPERIENCE with a Mandarin teacher in China was with a guy I'll call Eddie. I studied with about a dozen different tutors and teachers during our time in China and found there were two types, whom you can think of as professional and amateur. The pros, college-trained teachers of Chinese as a foreign language, all seemed cut from the same cloth. They were enthusiastic, practised and patient. They really knew their stuff technically: the grammar, the drills, the rhythms of a class. The amateurs, mainly freelance tutors, were more of a mixed bag of eccentric personalities and styles. It took a certain chemistry and meeting of minds between tutor and student for the interaction to work well. When the chemistry was right, the results could be great. I learned my most useful and practical "street language" from some of my amateur tutors.

Eddie was an amateur. I found him on Craigslist, which offers plenty of tutors to choose from. Eddie's CV showed that he had an unusual background, one in classics and linguistics, so I was intrigued. Unfortunately, there turned out to be a gap between the Craigslist Eddie and the real-life Eddie. (Surprise surprise!)

Real Eddie was rather puffed up about his scholarly background and dead set that I should learn exactly what he wanted to teach me. For my own good, he said, I needed to learn to talk about antiquities and Confucius. I told him that actually, it would be a lot more valuable to me to learn grammar and language for everyday life.

Ignoring me, Eddie pushed on: "How old is China?" he demanded. "China is 5000 years old," I answered, parroting part of an oft-heard catechism. Then he asked me the Chinese names for some other ancient countries besides China. I happened to know India (Yìndù), but stalled on Greece. "Xīlà," he said. (I should have known that one.) "How about Egypt?" he asked. Who would know this, I wondered. (It is Aijí.)

Eddie was starting to seem like a bully. "Mesopotamia?" he asked. I told Eddie flatly that I didn't want to learn how to say Mesopotamia in Chinese, because I would never remember it, and I didn't want to know how to say Sumeria either, because I would never have occasion to use it. He was not pleased. We both recognised a deadlock, and

Eddie looked relieved when I said I would "get back to him" about the next lesson.

It was a pity, because I think Eddie would have had a lot to teach me about the history of Chinese. It was clear that he, like many Chinese people, loved much about his country – its ancient history, its deep culture and the stories of its linguistic evolution. Eddie would probably love the account I stumbled across about John Webb, a seventeenth-century English architect and amateur scholar. Webb wrote about Stonehenge, and he also dipped his toe somewhat sloppily into the history of Chinese language. Webb argued that Chinese was the language of Adam and Eve in the Garden of Eden, the original language before the Tower of Babel, a hypothesis quite readily dismissed by others.

He produced a now quaint-seeming book on the subject (*see below*). I am sure that Eddie would have made good use of it.

A more accurate history of recent developments in the Chinese language would report that it took a sweeping turn in 1912, at the end of the imperial era and the founding of the Republic of China. It was apparent to the idealistic new leaders that the current language situation was dysfunctional as a backbone for a young, unified nation. They needed a change.

At that time, imperial court officials spoke a version of the Beijing dialect for governmental purposes, leaving masses of ordinary people and daily life across the vast reaches of the rest of the country awash in a soup of mutually unintelligible disparate languages and dialects. Only a thin slice of the highly educated elite mastered the written-only language, called Wenyan, or as we know it, classical or literary Chinese, a language of thousands of characters that largely lacked tenses, gender, grammar, and even prepositions, and which *no one actually ever spoke*. This was an extreme version of the Catholic Church's situation before the reforms of the 1960s, in which Latin was the official language, one that no parishioners actually spoke; the difference was that many ordinary Catholics at least understood the Latin Mass. China's situation effectively cut off the ordinary people from high literary culture. But, as China engaged with the outside world, intellectuals began to recognise that to pull their new country into the modern era, they needed to address both language issues: the spoken languages that varied so dramatically from region to region, and the written language that was inaccessible to all but a tiny elite. What followed was about four decades of confusing and emotional language debates, the linguistic element of the mass effort that began to pay off in unifying the country.

The question for the spoken language was: should China formally establish a single national language? On one side of the principled argument were those who said a national language would unify the country and help move it forward as a strong, more integrated modern republic. They were largely Beijingers, who knew that they had some advantages on their side: their northern dialect was more widely spoken than any other dialect and, since Beijing was the main cultural and intellectual centre, a variant of the Beijing dialect was the most logical candidate for such a "national language".

On the other side were those who said that choosing any one language was unfair; it would marginalise everyone who was not a native speaker of that language. Arguing this side were, for example, the Shanghainese, who feared the one-language solution (probably a derivative of Beijing Mandarin) could snuff out their own regional culture. The rivalry between Beijingers (*Běijīngrén*) and Shanghainese (*Shànghǎirén*) has long been both personal and bitter.

Then as now, Shanghai had bling, sophistication, commerce. Beijing had cultural power, history, the academy. Today, almost a century beyond the official language debates, I regularly hear the question: "Shanghai or Beijing, which do you like better?" It is a dreaded query, one that brings trouble no matter which way you answer it. Here is a typical scene of how the exchange plays out.

One nice Beijing morning, I went looking at apartments. I dreamed of moving from our sterile if convenient digs, and I called an agent who was showing an apartment in a funky old diplomatic compound. (Luckily for us, foreigners can now live just about anywhere they want to in China, a dramatic change from being restricted to a few designated housing compounds through the mid-1990s.) The agent was one tough young city woman. We got around to chatting about my having lived recently in Shanghai. In the middle of our conversation, she blurted out, "I hate Shanghai people!" I was taken aback and asked her why. "I don't know. I just hate them. I hate them all." I asked her then about Shanghai people: "Do they hate Beijing people?" "They hate everyone," she answered. Conversations like this were not rare.

Squabbling over the choice of a national language lasted a few decades. Interestingly, the Nationalists, who were in power first and later fled for Taiwan, and then the Communists, who followed them into power, both reached a consensus that a derivative of northern Mandarin spoken around Beijing (but which toned down some of the more identifiable markers of Beijing-speak, like the classic pirate-sounding "arrr" endings) would be the official language. The Nationalists called this Guóyǔ, "the national language". The Communists called it Pǔtōnghuà, "the common speech".

The debates and decisions about the written language were even more fundamental and consequential. In the exciting, infectious spirit of the new republican and post-May Fourth Movement era of the early 1920s, when the Chinese began to re-examine almost every aspect of their traditional culture, writers like the still-revered Lu Xun (who was by tradition a writer in classical Chinese but who switched his allegiance to the idea of a written language for the common people) were creative, daring and prolific. The new written language (often referred to as the "vernacular" in this context), was a much better match, grammatically and otherwise, with the way people actually spoke. It was called Báihuà, literally, "white language" or "plain language", and it made literature newly accessible to ordinary people. Mass-circulation magazines and newspapers were also born during this time, which gave many more ordinary people so much more to read besides what they had been used to – mostly just official notices and street signs!

There was another problem, however, because the Chinese character system, which was suited to ancient, unspoken literary Chinese, was a cumbersome match with the very different vernacular in which the new literature was being written – the language of everyday life.

As a solution, some writers and reformers began to believe that it was time for China to make the switch to a western-style alphabet, or some other phonetic writing system. (Korea's *hangul* and Japan's *hiragana* and *katakana*, for instance, have no relation to western alphabets but are logical and phonetic and fairly easy to learn.) Reformers pointed out various advantages of adopting a phonetic writing system. A phonetic alphabet, with agreed-on pronunciations for each letter or symbol, could help codify an "official" pronunciation of a new nationwide official language and could help kids learn "correct" pronunciation. Also, it could help more people learn to read and write more easily. (As it happened, the idea of official nationwide pronunciation was eventually abandoned, in the face of powerful, deep-rooted regional accents. Even in his day, Chairman Mao spoke with such a heavy Hunan accent that most of the Chinese masses he ruled simply couldn't understand him when he talked. It would be like forcing people from Mississippi to talk as if they were from Boston, or Liverpudlians to talk as if they were from London. Look how much trouble Henry Higgins had teaching one sharp little girl!)

Logic might seem to have been on the reformers' side. But the debates over a phonetic v. not-phonetic alphabet were fraught. The arguments – academic, political, social, linguistic, emotional, regional – were messy and angry. Every group had a bone to pick.

Which phonetic system was best designed; what should the symbols look like; whose pronunciation should be considered "standard"; who was on whose side? etc.

At one point, reflective of the chaos, one small group even suggested throwing the whole mess over in favour of Esperanto, the man-made language, which, they reasoned, would be less fettered for all in many ways.

Esperanto was quickly abandoned as a far-out idea, although staunch proponents of the language live on in China. Improbably enough, Esperanto provided the entrée for our family's first visit to China. We were living in Japan in 1986, and received an invitation to attend the World Esperanto Congress in Beijing, provided we could learn a little Esperanto first. So we patched together a few conversations and taught them to our kids:

Mi estas malsata. Cu estas ajo mangi?
I am hungry. Is there something to eat?

Cu ni estas en Hangzhou jam?
Are we in Hangzhou yet?

We learned enough, and for three weeks, we dragged around China with two busloads of Esperanto speakers from all over the world, including one little girl from New Zealand, who was the same age as our kids and whose parents were raising her as a native speaker of

Esperanto. (I always wondered what happened to her.) The group's sessions were conducted in Esperanto, but whenever a critical housekeeping detail arose, like what time the buses would roll in the morning, the speakers switched to English.

The arguments over a phonetic writing system droned on for decades. Different systems fell in and out of favour, but none really got traction. The old, impractical, but apparently impossible-to-replace character system lived on.

When the Communists came to power in 1949, Mao stamped his own imprints on the language reform movement. He dealt with the writing system in ways that he said would make it more accessible to the masses, and which critics (from the safety of decades later!) have often labelled a dumbing-down of the vaunted traditional linguistic system. These included a two-pronged approach. First, they shrank the vocabulary used in public media and official documents and propaganda, so ordinary people would have fewer characters to master in order to become literate. Second, they reduced the number of strokes needed to write thousands of the traditional complex characters (called *fántǐzì*), creating simplified characters (*jiǎntǐzì*). In addition, they finally adopted a phonetic alphabet called *Pīnyīn*, which (more or less) spells out the sounds of Chinese characters using Roman letters. To this day, mainland China uses simplified characters and Pinyin. An unforeseen bonus of Pinyin is its great flexibility for use on computer keyboards and in texting on mobile phones.

The language reforms of the twentieth century represented a massive, daunting linguistic engineering task. Languages are constantly changing, but normally they change slowly and organically, with less imposition and decree. These reforms, and many of their final implementations, represented something more like the sudden shift of tectonic plates during an earthquake, akin to the degree of the political and social shifts in China during the same time.

Today, the Mandarin Putonghua works pretty well as a national language. Most Chinese can understand it and speak it, although they may speak with a heavy accent and also may conduct many of their everyday affairs in their local dialect.[20] Some of the older generation and some ethnic minorities, like Uighurs, who are not educated in Putonghua, are still left out. Young Uighurs who make it to university even now have to pass a Mandarin test or study it remedially.

Here is a sense of the language varieties heard around China. Mandarin with regional accents: when speaking Mandarin, the Chinese can generally understand each

---

20 There is a fuzziness around the definitions of dialect and language. Generally, and for purposes here, dialects share more vocabulary with each other, more grammar, and are more likely to be mutually understood. Languages are farther apart in all these respects. For example, some people say Shanghainese (a Wu language) and Cantonese are dialects of Chinese; others says they are all separate languages.

other despite their heavy regional accents, which are as different as those of Brits, Aussies, Americans, Jamaicans and Nigerians when they are speaking English. Other Sino-Tibetan languages: more than 300 million Chinese speak another language besides Mandarin, including languages like Cantonese, Wu, Gan, Min, Hakka, Yue and Xiang. While these languages all belong to the same greater Sino-Tibetan language family that includes Mandarin, they can be as different from each other as French is from Spanish or Italian. Beyond Sino-Tibetan languages: even farther afield linguistically, many of China's 50-plus minority populations speak other languages, including many that are not Sino-Tibetan. For example, the Mongolians, the Uighurs and the Manchus all speak Altaic languages, which are closely related to Turkish and Korean. Then there are the smaller groups such as Bai, Miao and Yi, which are of various origins.

Out on the streets of China, this actual linguistic hodge-podge complicates life for Mandarin language learners like me. When I hailed a taxi in Shenzhen, in the far south of China bordering on Hong Kong, I couldn't exchange a single comprehensible word with the Cantonese-speaking driver. At first, I thought it was my own shortcoming, but my Chinese friends from Beijing told me they were in the same boat: Cantonese, with its different sound system, word order and lexicon, is as foreign to them as native speakers of Mandarin as

German is to me. (If they'd written notes to each other, of course, they would have understood each other fine, since they use the same version of the written Chinese language.)

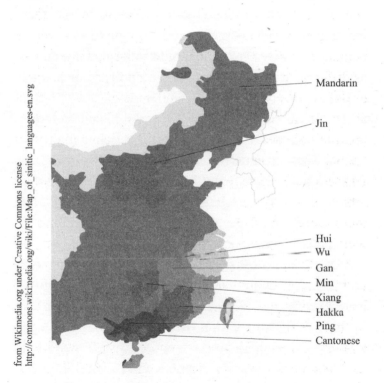

The major languages of eastern China

I tried for weeks – in vain – to talk with the regulars at my morning Shanghai tai chi practice. Eventually I realised with some embarrassment that it wasn't my poor Mandarin or what I took as their "heavy accents" that got in our way, but rather that they were speaking Shanghainese, a Wu language that is, again, about as similar to Mandarin as German is to English. My friend Ding, a Shanghai native, lives a bilingual day, flipping back and forth between Shanghainese and Mandarin, depending on what kind of business or errands she is doing.

Mandarin is reaching well beyond China now. It is starting to replace Cantonese as the lingua franca of Chinatowns around the world. Cantonese had been their traditional language because so many of China's earlier emigrants came from Cantonese-speaking areas in the south. In the US, Mandarin is taking off in popularity as a foreign-language study option, and the number of bilingual Mandarin-English primary schools is growing. While the visionaries in China's nascent republic 100 years ago might have been a little disappointed that there is still a polyglot of languages in 21st-century mainland China, they probably would have been surprised and heartened at its global reach.

Hànzì Characters

Chapter 11

The essence of being Chinese

ONE PAIR OF characters that pops up everywhere around China is 按摩, *ànmó*, which means massage. There it is on signs along a row of Shanghai's new-age spas on trendy Dagu Lu. Or scribbled by hand on cardboard scraps propped up along plaster walls in construction zones. Oversized signs with 按摩 appear in upper-storey windows of commercial buildings. Small signs are in backstreet barber shops that operate as hair cutteries by day and foot massage parlours by night. Massage is part of the menu at places like Beijing's slightly suspicious and rundown-looking No.1 Relaxing Club, which was right across from our apartment, or at the garish, Greek-temple-looking "waterworks" in the diplomatic neighbour-hood. And there is the blindman massage, 盲人按摩, the no-frills working-man's experience performed in modest surroundings by well-trained, state-subsidised blind people.

Blindman massage is my favourite, a cheap and easy tonic for a nerve-wracking day. If I was out on rounds of frustrating errands, I could just slip into the neighbourhood blindman massage parlour. There I lay down in a roomful of office workers on their furtive lunchtime breaks and weary shoppers taking a respite. We all came in buttoned up and stressed out, savoured our massages (while we were fully clothed), and then left, rumpled but mellow.

In the massage parlour, I liked catching glimpses of Chinese habits and real life: the blind man with his small electronic prompter, which beeped to announce the elapsed time; the male customers, unabashed and oblivious, easing into deep, rattling snores as they fully relaxed; the inane one-way conversations overheard on cell phones:

> *Client: Yeah, I'm having a massage now. (pause)*
> *Client: Oh, OK. OK, I can do that. (pause)*
> *Client: Carrots? Sure, how many? (pause)*
> *Client: In about an hour.*

Anmó looks like 按摩, sounds like "ahn muo". Most people will tell you they take more naturally to either the visual part or the oral part of Chinese, just like people take differently to music or art or sports. For me, I'll take listening and speaking over reading and – God forbid! – writing, no contest. Mastering characters seems impossible; I can practise a few characters for an entire week, trying to cram them into my brain. Then if I miss a few days, they have simply disappeared, as though never there in the first place. Conveniently, my husband is the yang to my yin. He has a lot of trouble with the sounds but says that the characters "make sense" to him. When we are out at a restaurant, he can look at the Chinese menu and say to me, "They have pork, or chicken, or noodles." And then I can ask the waiter for *zhūròu*, or *jī*, or *miàn*. We are a good team, a *dānwèi*.

Anmó, 按摩, is complicated to write in Chinese, taking 24 strokes to complete the two characters. But it is a useful example to help understand the puzzles and principles of how characters and words work in Chinese.

A Chinese word is generally written with one or two characters, occasionally three, like *lǎobǎixìng* 老百姓. Each character is pronounced as a single syllable. For example, the word for "wood, tree" is one syllable, *mù*, and is written with one character, 木, and sounds like "moo". The word "teacher" is two syllables, *lǎoshī*, and is written with two characters, 老师, and sounds like "lao sure".

Characters are constructed in several different ways. I am grateful for the simplest ones, like the character 人, *rén*, which means "person". This character has a single element, which carries both the meaning and sound rolled into one. And as a bonus, you can imagine that it looks like a little stick drawing of a person, which it originally was. If only characters were all so simple.

Other characters are composed of two parts. In many two-part characters, one part, called a radical, lends the character its meaning. Chinese has about 200 radicals, which carry general meanings like knife, person, strength, bowl, roof, grass, big, mountain, mouth, silk, horse, door, not, hand, wind, sick, field, rice, boat, bitter, walk, village, pig, rain, gold, ghost. The other part gives the character its sound.

For example, 汗 is the character for the word *hàn*, which means "sweat". The left part of the character, 氵 *shuǐ*, is the radical for "water", so if you can spot the radical 氵, you can guess that the character will have something to do with liquids, in this case "sweat".[21] The right part of this character, 干, is *gān*, and provides its sound, in the rhymed form *hàn* to the combined character. So, the two parts together create a new character, 汗, which means "sweat" and is said as "*hàn*".

Deconstructing characters can be a tough exercise and at best a vague guide to either meaning or

---

21 This radical form, 氵 *shuǐ*, water, never stands alone as a character, but always appears in combination with another piece to form a whole new character. The full form of the character 水, *shuǐ*, also means water, and it can stand alone as a word.

						mǎ	horse
						niǎo	bird
						guī	tortoise
						lóng	Chinese dragon
						fèng	Chinese phoenix

The evolution of characters from twelfth-century BC Oracle Bone script to current-day simplified script

pronunciation, but there is some detectable method to what often strikes me as complete madness.[22]

Massage, or *ànmó*, is a good example of how complicated a word and its characters can get. It is a two-syllable, two-character word. The first syllable, *àn*, is written as the character 按.

The radical 扌 is on the left side of this character, and it carries the general meaning of "hand", the hint that this character will mean something related to "hand".

---

22 Not all characters follow this pattern of meaning component + sound component. Sometimes there is no sound component. Sometimes there are two meaning components, etc. This is not a perfect science!

The right half of the character, 安, has two elements to it. The top half, 宀, means "roof", and the bottom half, 女, means "woman". Together, "woman under roof" is itself a character, 安 *ān*, meaning "peace", which is pronounced as "ahn". So, this right half of the character 安, gives the character, 按 the sound "ahn".

To summarise, in 按, the left part of the character 扌 means something about "hand", and the right part, 安 *ān*, sounds like "ahn". The new whole character 按, *àn*, has its own new meaning, "to press, as with fingers or thumb", and it is pronounced as "ahn".

That is half the battle. The second syllable of the word *ànmó*, massage, is 摩. The radical in this character is at the bottom, 手, and it also has the meaning of "hand". The top part provides the sound 麻, "má" (not exact, but close). It happens to mean "hemp" or "jute", but for this character, we're only interested in how it sounds.[23]

The entire second character with both its parts together is *mó*, pronounced as "muo" and has the meaning "to rub or touch". Again, the analysis isn't precise, but it at least has a vague connection to using your hand to rub or touch something. So finally, the new two-syllable, two-character word that means

---

23 This second character actually has three different radicals hiding in it. So, the first time you see this character, it's not easy to guess which is "the" relevant radical for this particular character.

massage is *ànmó*, 按摩. Phew! And that is one word, for one emotionally important but limited part of the day's rounds. When all is said and done, a lot of work goes into building characters. The explanations are often vague, but not entirely arbitrary.

Why do the Chinese hang onto this difficult character-based writing system? Characters are cumbersome; some have as many as seventeen strokes. They are hard to learn, and even Chinese adults will say they have to keep in practice to prevent getting rusty. They are awkward to look up in dictionaries; words are ordered first according to their radicals, and then by the total number of strokes it takes to draw the character.

Defenders of characters point out their merits. Many Chinese people respect characters for their ancient history and all the mysteries they embody. Today, the writing system works amazingly well to unite everyone in modern polyglot China. No matter what dialect they speak or how heavy their accent, all people can look at the same characters and derive the same meaning – even though they might pronounce the characters and words very differently. Chinese TV makes good use of this; nearly everything spoken on TV carries written subtitles. So TV watchers can cut through the differences of mutually unintelligible Mandarin, Cantonese or Shanghainese dialect, or heavy southern accents to read the same characters and "understand" what is being said. The Arabic numeral system works the same way.

Anyone in the world can look at "3" and know what it means, even though they may pronounce the numeral as three, *trois*, *drei*, *san*, etc. For speakers of other Asian languages, notably Japanese, the characters are a big advantage. Even though the grammar and structure of Japanese and Chinese, for example, are very different, the characters have similar meanings, so the Japanese can get a pretty good idea what signs, or names, or other writing means in China, and vice versa.

For the Chinese people, characters can also be a means to cut through the ambiguities of the spoken language. Chinese has so many homonyms, but each sound-alike word is represented by its own character with its own particular meaning. When Chinese people get stalled in a conversation and need to clarify a homonym, you often see the speaker scribbling out the shape of a character, "writing" on the palm of his or her hand with a finger if there's no pen or paper available, to illustrate its meaning to the listener.

As for the *ànmó*, the massages, I took advantage of every one that came my way. One stands out. My husband and I had just spent two long days with fresh-faced Chinese students at the Hunan Institute of Science and Technology in Yueyang. This is a tradition-bound place in central China, near the birthplace of Mao and still the heart of his most loyal following. The students were impressive in their English skills; English is one of the five compulsory topics on the viciously competitive nationwide university entrance exams, the *gāokǎo*, so all these kids, like those at other selective universities, had made the cut. During the first hour with the students, an interpreter translated our talks into Chinese. But he quickly retired, as it became clear that they were following everything we said.

After all the talking, all the picture-taking, all the dining and toasting, all the campus touring, our hosts presented us with university pins and red bound diplomas inscribed with honorary university degrees. They also invited us out into the cold rainy night for a communal foot massage.

So off we trooped with four or five distinguished university professors. Our destination, a glitzy glass and granite massage parlour that would have been at home in Las Vegas, belonged to a well-known chain. The giant building was ablaze against the dreary night, festooned with bright neon lights, an indoor palm tree theme, and an amusement park atmosphere. We climbed the wide staircase, past the tropical ferns and across watery lagoons, and entered a long, narrow room, where we flopped down side by side on massage beds in front of a blaring television.

The therapists arrived with buckets of scalding water for the rituals of foot washing. They parboiled our feet, swaddled them in hot towels, and prodded, pummelled and pinched. My feet looked normal, but my husband's feet looked like bright-red lobsters. A pedicurist arrived to address the toenails of the one woman professor, and another distinguished professor had his ears "candled", a (much-disputed) practice that claims to suction wax and debris from the ear canal by means of a hollow, burning candle inserted into the ear. It became midnight and beyond. My eyes were weeping from fatigue and the onset of a bad cold, *gǎnmào* 感冒. I wanted nothing more than to flee back to the (austere Mao-era, frigid) guest-house room and wrap myself in as many blankets as I could find. Our host insisted I felt bad only because my yin and yang were out of kilter, and that it was nothing a good session of cupping couldn't fix. Cupping is the millennia-old Taoist medical practice that aims to suck bad toxins out of the body. In a fog of fatigue and with a leap of faith, I agreed to try it.

I lay on my stomach as the therapist approached. He placed six small glass cups in two neat rows along my back. With a cigarette lighter, he created a fiery-icy vacuum, sealing the glass cups to my back. He didn't actually burn my skin; he lit a fire inside each of the cups, inverted as if they were light bulbs. Then as soon as the fire had used up the oxygen within the cup, he placed it down on my bare back, where the instantaneous vacuum sucked my skin about an inch deep into each cup. I saw a terrible shadow of apprehension cross my husband's face as he watched the skin from my back get pulled up into the glass cups.

The sensation was not unpleasant, and it did not rival the shock back in the government resthouse at 2:00am, when I peered over my shoulder into the mirror and saw six perfectly round, angry red welts, the size of small tangerines, across my back. After a numbing ten hours' sleep, I awoke with a start. Every trace of my cold was gone, and furthermore, although the welts have long since faded, I haven't caught a cold since. Once back in Shanghai, I began to notice all the young buff Chinese guys, and sometimes girls, at the gym, who were sporting tanktops designed to show off their cupping welts, clearly marks of some kind of pride.

I never gave much thought to massages before we went to China. But *ànmó* 按摩 took me by surprise. Both the written characters and the real-life event became symbolic to me, in a funny kind of way, of my China experience. The characters were difficult and complicated and I never could master them – just like everyday life in China. The massages themselves were curiously energising and humanly close to the *lǎobǎixìng*, the people – also like every day in China. Every time I go back to China, I will fondly return to the blind men to appreciate the modernising country's consideration for one of its most respected customs.

不可以

Bù kěyǐ   Not allowed

Chapter 12

Rules to follow and rules to break

ONE BLAZING HOT day in Shanghai, I was walking down a long street in search of an address that in the end I never did find. I paused for water and to rest for a minute on a low brick wall of a shopping mall plaza. Immediately, a guard came running over and cried hysterically, "*Bié zuò*!" "Don't sit there!" I jumped up, startled. It was another run-in with another rule. At the time, I still lacked the vocabulary to question why. So I picked myself up and shuffled dutifully along, hoping for luck at the next mall.

During our three years in China, I tried constantly to figure out the Chinese system of rules and regulations. There are so many rules of so many sorts, some transparent and others puzzling, some with good reason, others with no reason at all: no photos; no shoes; no entry; no swimming; no spitting. In Beijing, stand in line on the 11th of every month; in Shanghai, don't wear pyjamas outside (as Shanghai residents are wont to do!); no horn honking in school zones during the college entrance exam period. The rules are only randomly enforced, and the Chinese seem to have an inner compass about which rules to take seriously and which to ignore.

Cars pay no heed to green "walk" signals for pedestrians, just as pedestrians head blithely into the streets against red "don't walk" signals. Crowds ignore bus attendants who scream at them through their bullhorns to stand back from the kerbs. People argue with traffic wardens and even policemen who blast their whistles, trying in vain to keep people off the zebra stripes and safely on the pavements. Airline attendants warn passengers to stay buckled up until the plane arrives at the gate, but most passengers jump up to rummage through the overhead bins as soon as the wheels touch the runway. People smoke in front of no smoking signs, spit in front of no spitting signs, and sit on the grass in front of keep off the grass signs.

I watched my own behaviour gradually change during our time in China. Here are a few examples: I noticed that the gate guard at my neighbourhood public-housing compound would let me pass if I made no eye contact and aimed straight ahead for the laundry shop, but he would turn me back if I hesitated and looked as if I were asking for his OK. In a hurry another day, I bypassed the subway security, my bag in hand. No one paid attention, and from then on I gave up sending my things through any x-ray machines. Later, when my fully loaded transportation card didn't work, I shrugged my shoulders and sneaked under the turnstile. The subway attendants looked casually away. A bus conductor gave me a bye when I was a few cents short for the change box. I felt I was learning to shave the edges.

One day during the Beijing Olympic Games, I was inching through the long queues and the maze of security stops with a chocolate bar in my backpack. Destination: tennis matches. The people in front of me had all manner of chips, drinks and sweets abruptly confiscated. I was determined to save my chocolate bar, especially since the pickings for refreshments in the Olympic grounds were notoriously slim. I had been hoarding my chocolate bar for just this occasion. I figured if I was lucky, the guard might not recognise its characteristic triangle Toblerone shape. But the savvy guard spotted it and said "*Táng!*" "Sweets!" "*Bú shì táng*" "It's not sweets", I insisted. "*Zhè shì yào*" "It's medicine." "*Xūyào wǒ de yào!*" "I need my medicine!" I cried, taking a small bite. He paused with a look that suggested I would be more trouble than I was worth, and waved me through.

Why did I collaborate in petty flaunting of the rules, a national behaviour to which I had now become an accomplice? I wondered. Why does anyone (and everyone!) shave the rules in China?

The most convincing explanation I heard from my Chinese friends and China hands is that it is impossible to regard the rules in a way we consider "normal". There are two ways to read the facts: the arsenal of rules is so vast and so vague that no one can even reasonably keep track and obey them. Or, the arsenal of rules serves as a ready reserve in case the authorities might find it convenient to apply them. One of my young friends put it colloquially: there are so many rules that no one takes them seriously; they'll get you somehow if they want to. And, he added with a devilish tone, we break rules if we think we can, *just for the heck of it.*

To get my own gauge of which rules were flexible and when I might get away with breaking them, I began to study Chinese body language. There is the obvious body language we all recognise: the French are a bit haughty; Italians stand very close; Americans are always hugging; the Japanese cover their mouths and bow a lot.

There is a lot of learnable Chinese body language: don't hug; don't point; beckon with your fingers pointing down; girls hold hands with girls, and boys hold hands with boys; bow slightly (a derivative of kowtowing) when signalling respect; raise your folded hands up to your chest and give a few shakes to mean "good fortune"; when an audience applauds you, applaud back.

In Chinese, where much is spoken in a deliberately vague or indirect way, body language helps fill in the gaps. The Chinese are uncomfortable with an outright "no" in conversation, for example, and beat around the bush instead.

A posture, a look, a hesitation, or any one of a variety of subtle moves adds much to shades of meaning. This subtle kind of body language is not a teachable thing; you use your eyes and ears together to interpret a mismatch between what you're hearing and what you're seeing, or to catch a soft "I don't really mean it" undertone. Finally, you just get a feeling, and you know it when you see it.

I was walking along a roaring Beijing highway, heading for the pedestrian flyover to cross to the market in search of dinner. As I was about to take the first step up the concrete steps to the flyover, a skinny young soldier from the People's Liberation Army (PLA), in his oversized pea-green uniform and broad, tightly cinched belt, stepped right in front of me. He gathered himself into a ramrod-stiff pose and stern visage, as if to add a few authoritative years to his very tender-looking face. He planted himself midway across the first step and barked "No!" in fine English. His move was so sudden that I nearly tripped over him.

Pedestrians were walking back and forth over the flyover, up the steps, across the top, descending toward us, all indifferent to whatever rule he was trying to impose on me. Everything appeared normal. I asked, "*Wèishénme?*" "Why?"

The soldier shook his head a little and stood firm. I waved my arm upward, and wiggled two fingers as though they were walking. He shook his head again. I pointed to the people coming down the steps behind him. He waved me on in the direction of the next flyover, which was a good quarter-mile down the road, meaning an extra half-mile backtrack to the market.

By this point, a small crowd of other pedestrians who also wanted to cross the flyover had built behind me. It never takes long to build a crowd in China. One woman began scolding the soldier, as a mother might scold her son. (There is surprisingly little deference toward people in uniform in China.) Others joined in the complaining. The young soldier, visibly weakening in resolve, shuffled from one foot to the other. Then he moved slightly to one side and waved us through.

"*Wèishénme?*" "Why?" I asked the woman behind me this time, the self-appointed ringleader of our impatient group. She just looked at me, with an expression that might have said, "Why do you even ask?" She shrugged, and said in slightly accented English, "No reason."

I saw more body language another day, when my husband and I headed for the Cultural Palace of the Minorities to see an exhibit about the history and future of Tibet. We guessed it would be an interesting propaganda experience. There was a long queue for entry, and an unusual squadron of security guards at the ticket booth. Tibet is always a sensitive topic, and they were probably anxious about potential protests.

The guards asked for our passports. This was disappointing, because we never carried them. The laws say foreigners should carry passports, but the risk of loss or theft never seems worth the risk of violating this seemingly unenforced rule. Not once in more than two years in China had we been randomly asked for passports. My husband managed to produce his American driver's licence, but I had nothing with a photo. I tried my Visa card. No good. My subway card. They laughed.

But then I saw the guard shuffle gently, and I sensed wiggle room. It would be easier on both of us if he could find a way to let me pass without a fuss. I pulled out a magnetic key card, and mumbled a few things about it being to my apartment in Beijing. "*Wǒ Běijīng jiā de!*" "My Beijing house!" Everyone I dealt with on the streets of Beijing seemed to like it when I could produce some evidence that I actually lived there – a card, an address, my mobile phone, a little jabber in Mandarin. And *jiā* 家, which means both "family" and "home", is a wonderful word with cultural strength. Preposterously, my key card was a good enough substitute for my passport, and he let us through.

These are examples of petty transgressions, of course. There is also the serious issue of laws, enforcement and consequences at play in China. A backbreaking number of rules course through people's personal lives and define how they live: the one-child policy, enforced most everywhere except in certain rural areas and otherwise sanctioned with steep fines;[24] the home town registration system (*hùkǒu*) hitched to social welfare benefits like medical care and education. When city planners or real-estate tycoons decide that it's time to raze a block or neighbourhood to make room for something new, people who have made their lives in those places are shooed away, with a minimum of notice, choice or compensation. If you have guests in your home for more than a few nights, you must register their names with the police. In schools located south of the Yangtze River, no indoor heating is allowed, since they are theoretically in a "warm" part of China. This area notably includes Shanghai, with its climate roughly like that of Washington DC or London.

There are "in trouble if you don't, and in trouble if you do" rules. Before the Beijing Olympic Games, China's officials announced proudly to the world that they would accommodate peaceful protestors in "authorised protest" zones specially set up during the Games. This would demonstrate China's confident openness while on the international stage. But not only were all permissions to protest denied, some of the few brave souls who actually applied for permits were arrested.

---

24 The one-child policy has become a bit more wobbly and vague recently.

There are the cases where following the rules would have born good consequences. For many years, Beijing banned wildly popular private firework displays during the Chinese New Year holidays, because of the danger from explosions and possibly fires. In 2006, the ban was mostly eased, with some restrictions and some permissions required. Having witnessed a scary midnight celebration in 2008, our first year in Beijing, I for one would strongly endorse reinstating that unpopular ban. On that occasion, people were shooting industrial-size fireworks on the streets without regard for bystanders; burning embers rained down on sidewalks; trees caught fire. During New Year celebrations a year later, things got worse. Gala fireworks were set off next to the famous CCTV tower building in central Beijing (stories on permissions varied). The just-completed 40-storey Mandarin Oriental luxury hotel next door caught fire and burned to a crisp. The rule of thumb that has evolved around laws in China, "ask not for permission, but for forgiveness", certainly came up short in this instance.

During our time in China, I was well aware that we were frequently breaking rules – intentionally or accidentally – both legal rules and cultural rules; rules we were aware of and probably rules we never knew existed. Breaking rules in China was an interesting contrast to breaking rules in Japan, where we had also lived for a few years, many years ago. In Japan, I felt as though the Japanese were lying in wait for us, confident that they would catch a misstep. (Which they did! Again, there were so many rules, and the learning curve was steep.) In China, I felt as though we were in collusion with the people, the *lǎobǎixìng*, in face of some larger authority.

Although spoken Chinese was too nuanced for me to manage in the subtle world of rules and rule-breaking, I have discovered that the body language of Chinese – the shrugs, the looks, the shuffling – go a long way indeed as cues to understanding the parameters of a situation. Learning to read those cues became as important to me for our life in China as all the learning of the grammar and vocabulary of spoken Chinese.

地震

Dìzhèn Earthquake

Chapter 13

Out of calamity, tenderness

ONE FINE SPRING day in Beijing, I was working on my laptop in our 21st-floor apartment. I suddenly felt dizzy and light-headed, and gripped the edge of my desk, wondering if I might faint. Then the curtain pulls began to sway, and the walls began to creak, and the floor felt wobbly. It was Monday, May 12, 2008, at exactly 2:28pm, and a major earthquake was thundering through the mountains in rural Sichuan Province, 1000 miles to the southwest.

No phones rang, no alarms sounded, no one knocked on our door. I Googled "earthquake China" and within several minutes, there was a report from Reuters that the US Geological Survey had noted an earthquake in central China. An English-language China blog, Danwei. org, posted the first shreds of information at 2:47pm, not even twenty minutes after the earthquake had begun. Very soon there followed in the always-hyperactive

Chinese blogosphere a flurry of text messages, twitters, emails and personal comments about the earthquake.

The state-run television networks were slow to warm up to coverage, as if not sure how big or small they were supposed to play the emerging news, but by Tuesday, the incalculable damage and almost unimaginable human drama riveted me and most everyone else in China to the TV and would do so for the next seven days.

News began dribbling in with barebones reports from Chengdu, the nearest major city to the quake's epicentre. We saw the first scenes of devastation. As the week wore on, the most compelling moments were the raw human ones, with survivors and desperate parents watching and waiting in the shambles of Sichuan schoolyards. Even newscasters struggled to keep composure. I grabbed my dictionaries and searched as fast as I could for the words I didn't understand to fill in gaps and piece together fragments of meaning.

There was something unusual about the TV programming and the TV language during early coverage of the earthquake. The programming was ragged and unpolished, and the language was unrehearsed and plainspoken, more like normal street chatter. This was a far cry from the usual carefully scrubbed-and-scrutinised productions, with their official jargon and heavy words. Everyone agreed, at least at the beginning, that the government was allowing "unprecedented transparency" in media coverage.

My list of new words grew. Some of them came up over and over again.

> dìzhèn (*earthquake*); zāihài (*calamity*); ānwèi (*comfort*); yǒnggǎn (*brave*); jiù (*save*); liǎojiě (*understand well*); ānpái (*plan*); kào (*depend on*); jīhuì (*chance*); huīfù (*recover*); jīnglì (*energy*); bēi (*to carry on one's back*)

Some of the words began to assemble into a curious collage, highlighting one thing about the Chinese people that was new to me, and another that confirmed something I already suspected.

The first was about the tender side of the Chinese, a side normally kept well hidden. These are the words:

> ānwèi (*comfort*); kào (*depend on*); bēi (*to carry on one's back*); liǎojiě (*understand well*); zāihài (*calamity*)

After nearly two years of living in China, I had built up a stockpile of everyday experiences that I would describe as anything but tender. Getting through a day meant routinely being scared off sidewalks by bicycles, strong-armed into or out of crowded elevators, edged out of a seat on the bus by hale young men, jostled aside in any queue of any sort. I had to bargain (or at least try to get a fair price) for everything from vegetables to socks. I regularly dodged balls of spit as people cleared their throats and shot out phlegm, oblivious to others around them. I often saw screaming arguments over fender-benders, and the occasional brawl on street corners in respectable parts of town.

I grew used to a China that I thought of as rough and harsh. With newly honed instincts, I began to move through my day on-guard, elbows out, eyes scanning, and comfortable playing both defence and offence. It wasn't about physical danger, which I never for a single moment felt in China. Instead, it was about the bruising, wearing, embattling encounters of simply getting through everyday life, with so many people who all seemed to want to be just slightly in front of wherever I happened to be.

Of course, there are exceptions and tender moments in China. Everyone loves little children, and dotes on them. Most people also love pets, especially small dogs and birds. Some young people apparently still get lectures on chivalry toward their elders. On one red-letter day, I was running for a stopped taxi, just ahead of a downpour. Approaching in a run from the opposite direction was a teenage schoolboy, sporting a bright new-school-year-red Young Pioneer's scarf tied around his neck. He saw me, abruptly stopped, and in an almost-Elizabethan gesture, gallantly bowed and waved me into the taxi. It was a remark-able moment.

But overall, tender was not a word I needed to learn. So I was surprised when I caught wind of something like it in the national reaction to the earthquake.

Ānwèi 安慰, meaning "comfort", was a new word to me. I listened to a TV reporter describing the arrival of Premier Wen Jiabao in Sichuan. He was going to the ravaged towns to *ānwèi*, to comfort the people. Premier Wen often appears with children on TV or in photographs, and he always looks comfortable around them. "Grandfather Wen", they call him.

Maybe I was fooled, but even to my seasoned, sceptic's eye, I caught nothing in this footage that looked staged to me. Wen balanced on one knee, eye

Premier Wen Jiabao comforting a young earthquake victim

to eye with the children, and comforted them. The children were crying hard, not just whimpering, but sobbing with their whole small bodies. Wen enveloped them in his arms, instinctively, and said, "*Bié kū, bié kū.*" "Don't cry. Don't cry." He knelt there for longer than he needed for a photo op, until the children had quieted down. He was wearing sneakers, and when reporters tried to cover a little slip-and-stumble he took in the rubble, he abruptly brushed them off, reproaching them for diverting attention from the real mission at hand.

All that week, I would watch the strong tend the weak. Policemen guided weather-beaten farmers down the mountain paths. "*Xièxie xièxie. Gǎnxiè gǎnxiè gǎnxiè.*" "Thank you thank you thank you thank you," the old people nodded and repeated, over and over and over again, because it seemed they just couldn't say it enough. The hapless were *kào*, depending on the strong.

Firefighters carried the injured, often as big or heavy as they were themselves. Soldiers carried old people, a generation that looked so tiny and fragile compared to the taller, and sometimes even strapping youth of today's better-fed China. Teenagers carried small children, and small children carried smaller children.

The very curious image in this footage was the profile of the carrying: everyone, from soldier to young child, was carrying someone on his back. In America, this "piggyback" posture is usually part of field-day games. But in Sichuan, this style is still pervasive.

Bēi 背, "to carry on your back". When I asked my Chinese friends about it, they said, "Oh yes, that's how you do it in Sichuan. The terrain is hilly and treacherous and steep. You're usually on mountain paths, and the only way to carry is on your back. That's the way Sichuan people do it. *Bēi*."

Sure enough. Back on the streets of Beijing, I began to notice how many people carried so many things. One of my friends told me that the Chinese hate to pay to transport anything they could theoretically carry by themselves, and I saw a lot of evidence to support her point. On holidays, people carry the cheap, classic plaid plastic suitcases – ubiquitous in the Third World – on the trains and buses. Migrant workers sling old grain bags, now bursting with quilts and personal belongings, over their shoulders. Farmers in from the countryside balance pails or baskets on wooden yokes across their shoulders. Sometimes women from the countryside carry baskets of cherries on their heads. In the middle of 2008, when plastic bags first went from being free to costing a few cents each, I saw a young woman run across nine lanes of traffic, carrying her groceries awkwardly wrapped up in her jacket. She tripped, the jacket undid, and cans and jars went rolling everywhere.

People watched and chuckled, some in sympathy but others, I fear, just because they were amused. After

Sichuan peasant carrying a market basket on her back

years of living in Beijing, I was no longer surprised
to see people openly laugh and point at dwarves or
very tall people, or gawk and giggle at crippled children doing acrobatics as a form of begging on the
streets of Shanghai. Some say the giggles are signs of
embarrassment and that staring is just a sign of curi-
osity; it looked more like simple heartlessness to my
foreigner's eye. The week after the earthquake was
different; I saw a stranger's arm around a shoulder,
a "there but for the grace of God" look in people's

eyes. I wondered if a new word I learned, *liǎojiě*, fit these images.

Liǎojiě means "to understand". The shade of meaning covers slightly different terrain from the other words for "understand". There is *míngbai*, which is more like "I get it"; *zhīdào*, which is more a "know, as in fact"; *rènshi* means "know, as in to be acquainted". *Liǎojiě* goes deeper. The second character, *jiě* 解, in *liǎojiě* 了解, means to "untie" or "undo", evoking the sense of deeper understanding that comes from working to untie or resolve something bound and "knotty".

The rescuers in the earthquake zone certainly had a genuine compassion for the victims of the disaster. It was easy to imagine that they *liǎojiě*, or understood, the situation a little more deeply from bearing such close witness. In China, I was constantly amazed at the difficult personal histories people would reveal to me. One by one came the Cultural Revolution dramas of rustication as a teenager, or families blown apart in the political chaos, or shattering betrayals by neighbours and good friends. It was like talking with Europeans about what had happened during the 1930s and 1940s. Most of today's Chinese people had not even been born when the Cultural Revolution was under way. Still, I thought there might be something in the recent national memory, a memory of mass vulnerability, that brought forward empathy during such a calamity, *zāihài*, as the earthquake.

I also learned some words that confirmed something I had already guessed about the Chinese: they persevere. Six thousand miles of the Long March, five years of the Great Leap Forward, then the endless Cultural Revolution, and today's lifetimes still spent in tough factories and on medieval-like farms.

yǒnggǎn (*brave*); jīnglì (*energy*); jīhuì (*chance*); ānpái (*plan*); jiù (*save*); huīfù (*recover*)

"If there is only one per cent chance, we will continue looking." *Jīhuì*, chance. This was the phrase on everyone's tongues for nearly a week after the earthquake. In the beginning, the soldiers marched through the night, spurred by Wen Jiabao's order to reach the epicentre by midnight Tuesday, not even 36 hours after the quake occurred. Then they continued marching, higher into the mountains, dragging supplies and equipment toward the remote villages. Then they found the people and carried them down the mountains. Over and over again.

Theirs was not *yǒnggǎn*, to be brave in the wartime sense, requiring a moment's heroism under fire, but rather their strength demonstrated an irrepressible, elementary *jīnglì,* energy.

Early in the week of the earthquake, rescuers dug with their bare hands. There were no steam shovels, or even hand shovels, picks or axes. They clawed out bricks; they passed armfuls of metal rebar and stacks of splintered wood along a human chain, one by one from the top of a heap to the bottom.

The sun went down, the klieg lights beamed on, and the work continued. They heaved slabs of concrete on cue, and even if you didn't know how to count in Chinese, you would understand: *Yī, èr, sān … Yī, èr, sān …*

How to plan, *ānpái*, this massive rescue? It was simple: the rescuers would keep on until there was nothing more. They portaged boats. They clambered over rocks. They parachuted out of helicopters. They kept digging into the rubble of fallen buildings or the landslide-covered houses. There were three days of miracles, as rescuers pulled one person after another out from the mangled debris. They saved so many lives. *Jiù*, to save.

Then things slowed down and success stories only trickled in: someone was found alive after 160 hours, more than six days. It was impossible not to calculate all that one does in six days – the meals you eat, the work you do, the hours you sleep, the chores. There was another survivor after 176 hours, and another at 179. Then they found another after 195 hours. Finally, impossibly, a woman was pulled from the debris after 216 hours. She was the last. After nine days, the rescuers stopped looking for survivors. For Sichuan to recover, *huīfù*, would take a long, long time.

My list of words learned in the aftermath of the earthquake told me a story in staccato about the Chinese, one of both tenderness and perseverance.

很好

Nǐ de Zhōngwén hěn hǎo!   Your Chinese is really good!

Chapter 14

A little goes a long way

HOW HARD IS it to learn Chinese, really?

I was flipping through the channels on Chinese TV one day, and I paused at a travel programme for Chinese tourists about Spain. It was partly in Spanish and partly in Chinese. I watched for a while and then realised, a bit heartsick, that after two years of being in China, I could understand more Spanish than Chinese – and the closest I had ever come to studying Spanish was French!

Language teachers and linguists generally agree that Chinese is one of the world's most difficult languages for English speakers to learn, along with several others, like Japanese, Russian and Arabic.

I ran into plenty of testimonials supporting that notion. Sometimes the vexation is about holding onto what you drum into your head week after week. One of my first classmates was a young Norwegian woman who was fluent in lots of languages and was a star in our class. One day, she returned to class from being off sick for a week and was uncharacteristically completely tongue-tied. After stumbling a few times, she switched to English and blurted out: "It is *astonishing* how quickly I forget!"

A guy who worked for an American magazine in Beijing was recounting his erratic, unsystematic progress in Chinese. He said he felt proud when he randomly spotted – and understood – a written Chinese character he had been studying for weeks. But on the other hand, he said he frequently fell into despair when he couldn't come up with the simplest kinds of phrases, like "I can't find my shoes".

And another student of Chinese confessed to me that for him the difficulty was all about accent. His Chinese friends, who were always encouraging him, said it would help if he would give them a heads-up before he spoke: "Just let us know when you're speaking in Chinese, OK?"

I personally found it most perplexing that so little about Chinese resonated with any other language I had ever worked on. Chinese seemed so arbitrary, and there was nothing to grab onto. I could try to memorise the same words two or three or four times over, only to have them slip away again. It probably took a good eighteen months before I pummelled enough into my head to accumulate a critical, usable mass of vocabulary, or to say something without rehearsing it, or to pick up story plots, or to understand conversations I overheard on the street, or accomplish more than the simplest transaction. Approaching any sense of intuition about the language was painfully slow. For me, Chinese is *that* hard.

Chinese dishes out a heavy dose of visual and oral demands, starting with the burdens of characters and tones. Mastering a new word involves several steps. Learning even an easy word like *shì* (to be) means remembering more than that it sounds like "sure". This is the *shì* with the falling tone, not shī, shí, shǐ (with high tone, rising tone and falling-rising tone, respectively) or *shi* with no tone at all. And it also means learning that among the homonyms of *shì* with the same falling tone, this *shì* is represented by the character 是, not 市 (market); 士 (scholar); 事 (thing, affair); 视 (look at, regard); 试 (try, test), to name just a few of the others.

All this makes for very slow progress, in a country where life moves very fast. In my real China life, every step I took was about getting things done and surviving the day: How do I buy tickets to Chengdu? Who is on the phone and what are they asking me? Which exit do I take? Tomorrow is a holiday? Is this chocolate or red-bean paste? Where is the vegetable market? Uh oh, this is the toilet? How much should I pay? Is this ice in my drink safe? How do I work the TV remote? The internet is out; no taxi will stop here; the bank card isn't working; this zipper needs repair; we are out of ibuprofen; I need a haircut; these plugs don't fit; all the shoes in China are too small for me; there is no building at this address; but the sign says "open"; and well, the repair guy fixing my shoes was on this corner yesterday ...

There are tried-and-true ways to learn another language – be young, stick with consistent classes, immerse yourself in the speaking situation. But life doesn't always work out in one of these ways, so you have to ad lib. I can finally look back (and look ahead!) at the trial and error of my pursuit of Chinese to see what worked for me and what didn't.

I learned to triage and lean toward my strengths. That means relying on my ears rather than my eyes. Most people will tell you they do better with either the visual or the oral parts of Chinese. For me, hearing the language and trying to speak it is much easier than seeing the characters and trying to recognise them, let alone write them. So I focus on what I can hear and say. My husband is just the opposite: he can recognise and remember the characters but has a much harder time hearing or saying differences in words. My theory is that having one linguistic strength or the other is like being right-handed or left-handed; you're just born that way. As pathetic as I feel about my shortcomings with characters, I do find some solace in the fact that keeping up with characters is a lifelong pursuit even for the Chinese.

Several of my Chinese friends admitted that, if they let difficult characters go too long, they get rusty about remembering them.

I would have loved to start at the beginning of my Chinese study with a solid classroom programme and go on systematically from there. But the logistics of our China life meant we were always on the move, travelling a lot, with no set schedule. Since it was hard to maintain regular school schedules, I mixed it up. At different times, I studied in commercial schools, hired tutors, watched lots of TV, followed online courses and podcasts, listened to the radio talk shows and Chinese songs, watched Chinese movies, killed time in queues or on the subway listening to other people's conversations. Everything helps. The personal situations worked best; those Westerners with Chinese boyfriends or girlfriends learned the quickest. For the rest of us, we found language substitutes. Chinese love having "language partners" where you swap Chinese and English practice with a partner. I found a few matches that worked out well, when we could spend hours and hours chatting about this, that and everything. What we lacked in grammatical progress, we more than made up for in useful and funny conversation.

Whenever I could, I also listened to little children, with their deliberate pronunciation, simple words and context-heavy jabber. I wish I could turn back the clock to have a child's pliable brain – easier to get those accents, and the enviably effortless-seeming acquisition. Alas. On the other hand, the news is not all bad. Being older and more linguistically experienced means you can intellectualise your way through some learning, like recognising language structure or patterns (for example, if adjectives precede or follow the nouns they modify, or if verbs come before or after the object of a sentence), which make the learning process more efficient. And you can find great gratification, which I craved and desperately needed to survive China, when you say something simple like "*Shūdiàn zài nǎr?*" "Where's the bookstore?" and someone will answer – with misplaced and generous praise – "*Nǐ de Zhōngwén hěn hǎo!*" "Your Chinese is very good!"

For me, chipping away at the language not only made China more survivable, it also tipped the daily balance even ever-so-slightly from being an observer to being a participant in the fray and chaos of developing China. I can't believe I am quoting Chairman Mao, but he actually said something very good that applies to me! "*Hǎohǎo xuéxí, tiāntiān xiàngshàng*". This is literally "Good good study study, day day up". Or, more comprehensibly, "Study hard, and you will improve every day." Practice makes perfect. These are words I live by in China.

I did inch away from being overwhelmed at such a massive, intense, overwhelming country, toward touching a few people one by one, and getting a little closer to their lives, however small the increment. This reward gave me at least the illusion that I belonged, if just for a little bit, in this extraordinary country at this moment in history.

A guide to pronunciation

This is a rough guide to help you sound out the Chinese words. In many regions of China, there will be variations on these pronunciations.

ə is the sound of the "a" in the word "about", or the "e" in "taken", or the "i" in "pencil". In phonetic terms, it is called schwa.

ō is the long "o" sound, like the "o" in "no" or "toe".

zh sounds similar to the "j" sound in "edge", but the tip of the tongue touches a little farther back on the roof of the mouth.

ao is the vowel sound in "now", "how" and "Mao".

ai is the vowel sound in "hi", "my" and "eye".

ü as a sound in English is closest to "u" in "unit" or "use". It appears in German words, as in "*über*" or French as in "*sucre*".

Chapter 1
wǒ ài nǐ = wō ai nee
Uighur = wee gər
Xīnjiāng = sheen jyahng
zuótiān = dzwō tyen
chànggē = chahng gə
zài = dzai

Chapter 2
bú yào = boo yao
zuótiān = dzwō tyen
jīntiān = jeen tyen
míngtiān = ming tyen
hòutiān = hō tyen
bú yòng = boo yōng
méi yǒu = may yō
bú shì = boo shər
bù kěyǐ = boo kə yee
xià chē = shyah chə
wèi = way
fúwùyuán = foo woo yü en
màn zǒu = mahn dzō
gěi wǒ yán = gay wō yen
qǐng = ching

xièxie = shyeh shyeh
zuò = dzwō
xiū = shyō
máfan = mah fahn
kàn = kahn
yi = yee
mǎ = mah
zǒu = dzō
wánr = wahr

Chapter 3
shī, shí, shǐ, shì = shər
nǐ = nee
hǎo = hao
ma = mah
kuài = kwai
chī = chə
fàn = fahn
mǐfàn = mee fahn
Pǔtōnghuà = poo tōng hwah
Hànyǔ = hahn yü
Zhōngwén = zhōng wen
xiàngshēng = shyahng shəng
sì = sə
bā = bah
fā cái = fah tsai
zhōng = zhōng
fú = foo

dào = dao
chéngyǔ = chung yü
shǒu zhū dài tù = shō zhoo dai too
xiàn xué xiàn mài = shyen shüeh shyen mai
xīn = sheen
xīnnián = sheen nyen
de = də
kāi = kai

Chapter 4
dǎbāo= dah bao
huānyíng guānglín = hwahn ying gwahng leen
qípáo = chee pao
yǒu = yō
hóng = hōng
yóuyǒng = yō yōng
jiǔ bā = jyō bah

Chapter 5
lǎobǎixìng = lao bai shing
tóngzhì = tōng zhə
tóngzhìmen = tōng zhə mən
Chóngqìng = chōng ching
Guǎngdōng = gwahng dōng
rénmínbì = rən meen bee

Chapter 6
Nǐ hǎo = nee hao

Wǒ jiào = wō jyao
Mínyì = meen yee
Fāng Fēi Jié = fahng fay jyeh
jiè bǐ = jyeh bee
Wáng Míng Yuán = wahng ming yü en
Wèixīng = way shing
Zhèn shēng = zhen shəng
Aoyùn = ao yün
Yǒnghóng = yōng hōng
Jiànguó = jyen gwō
Àipíng = ai ping
Jiànmín = jyen meen
Shèbǎo = shə bao
Mínyì = meen yee
Héxié = hə shyeh
Fènduī = fənd way
Guǎngzhōu = gwahng zhō
Shēnzhèn = shen zhen
Chén = chən
lǎoshī = lao shər
Huáng Hùshi = hwahng hoo shə
Lǐ Yīshēng = lee yee shəng
Zhāng Sījī = zhahng sə jee
Zhōu Shīfu = zhō shə foo
gēge = gə gə
mèimei = may may
ōu bā mǎ = ō bah ma
ào bā mǎ = ao bah mah

fēi ěr pǔ sī = fay ayr poo sə
bù shí = boo shər
lǐ gēn = lee gən (hard g as in reagan)
shā shì bǐ yà = shah shə bee yah
luò shān jī = lwō shahn jee
niǔ yuē = nyō yü eh
hǎo lái wù = hao lai woo
Shānxī = shahn shee

Chapter 7
dōngběi = dōng bay
xī běi = shee bay
dōngnán = dōng nahn
jiǎo = jyao
xià = shyah
shàng = shahng
lóu = lō
fēijī = fay jee
shān = shahn
Xiàmén = shyah mən
zhuōzi = zhwō dzə
shàng ge Xīngqī èr = shahng gə shing chee ahr
yuè = yü eh
cì = tsə
fēngshuǐ = fəng shway
Shěnyáng = shən yahng
Chéngdū = chung doo
Urumqi = oo ruhm chee

Hángzhōu = hahng – zhō
Nánjīng = nahn jing
Kūnmíng = kuhn ming
Bówùguǎn zài nǎr = bō woo gwahn dzai nahr
xiè xie = shyeh shyeh

Chapter 8
Xizhou = shee zhō
Liang = lyahng
gāokǎo = gao kao
xiāngxìn = shyahng sheen
zìjǐ = dzə jee

Chapter 9
rènao = rə nao
xiǎoxīn = shyao sheen
kāixīn = kai sheen
fàngxīn = fahng sheen
shāngxīn = shahng shccn
rèxīn ‾ rə shccn
mótè = muo tə
qiǎokèlì = chyao kə lee
shālā = shah lah
luómàn = lwō mahn
luóji = lwō jee
yīn yáng = yeen yahng
kāiguān = kai gwahn
hǎohuài = hao hwai

duōshǎo = dwō shao

hūxī = hoo shee

zuǒyòu = dzwō yō

dōngxi = dōng shee

gāoǎi = gao ai

dàxiǎo = dah shyao

diàn = dyen

diànhuà = dyen hwah

diànnǎo = dyen nao

diànshì = dyen shər

diàntī = dyen tee

diànyǐng = dyen ying

diànbào = dyen bao

diànchē = dyen chə

chē = chə

fùmǔ = foo moo

yǔmào = yü mao

míngbai = ming bai

yānhóng = yen hōng

niánqīng = nyen ching

tiānqì = tyen chee

huǒchē = hwō chə

mǎmahūhū = mahmah hoohoo

mǎshàng = mah shahng

xìngfú = shing foo

xiàtiān = shyah tyen

Chapter 10
tīng bù dǒng = ting boo dōng
Yìndù = yeen doo
Xīlà = shee lah
Āijí = ai jee
Běijīngrén = bay jing rən
Shànghǎirén = shahng hai rən
Guóyǔ = gwo yü
Pǔtōnghuà = poo tōng hwah
Lǔ Xùn = loo shün
Báihuà – bai hwah
fántǐzì = fahn tə dzə
jiǎntǐzì = jyen tə dzə
Pīnyīn = peen yeen

Chapter 11
hànzì = hahn dzə
zhūròu = zhoo rō
jī = jee
miàn = myen
dānwèi = dahn way
ànmó = ahn muo
Dagu Lù = dah goo loo
mù = moo
lǎoshī = lao shər
rén = rən
hàn = hahn
shuǐ = shway

gān = gahn
má = mah
Yuèyáng = yüeh yahng
gāokǎo = gao kao
gǎnmào = gahn mao

Chapter 12
bù kěyǐ = boo kə yee
bié zuò = byeh dzwō
bú shì táng = boo shər tahng
zhè shì yào = zhə shə yao
xūyào wǒ de yào = shü yao wō də yao
wèishěnme = way shen mə
wǒ Běijīng jiā de = wō bay jing jyah də
jiā = jyah
hùkǒu = hoo kō

Chapter 13
dìzhèn = dee zhən
zāihài = dzai hai
ānwèi = ahn way
yǒnggǎn = yōng ahn
jiù = jyō
liǎojiě = lyao jyeh
anpái = ahn pai
kào = kao
jīhuì = jee hway
huīfù = hway foo

jīnglì = jing lee
bēi = bay
Wēn Jiābǎo = wen jyah bao
bié kū = byeh koo
gǎnxiè = gahn shyeh
míngbai = ming bai
zhīdào = zhə dao
rènshi = rən shə
Yī, èr, sān = yee ahr sahn

Chapter 14

Nǐ de = nee də
Zhōngwén = zhōng wen
hěn hǎo = hen hao
shūdiàn zài nǎr = shoo dyen dzai nahr
hǎohǎo xuéxí, tiāntiān xiàngshàng = hao hao shüeh
shee tyen tyen shyahng shahng

Acknowledgements

When my husband, Jim, and I left Washington DC for Shanghai, we knew only a handful of the people mentioned below. We didn't know a single soul in China. (A stunning fact, when you think that there are 1.3 billion people in China!) By the time we returned to the US three years later, each and every one of these people had become near and dear to us. We might have survived China without them, but only barely. I thank them all for their help in their individual, generous ways.

In Shanghai: Dean Ding, Jessica Dong, Michelle Garnaut, Dan Guttman and ZeeZee Zhong, York-Chi and Stephen Harder, Andrew Houghton, Ken and Ann Jarrett, Kitty Leung, Ben Liotta, Isaac Mao, Adam Minter, John Northen, Lucia Pierce, Liz Rawlings and Steve Chalupsky, Andy Rothman and Robin Bordie, Anne-Marie Slaughter and Andy Moravcsik, Kyle Taylor, Louis Woo, Jarrett and Candice Wrisley.

In Beijing: Fr. Ron Anton, Andrew Batson, Bing and Dan Bell, Weilian Carter, Chen Xin, Duncan Clark,

Susan Conley and Tony Kieffer, Melanie and Eliot Cutler, Simon Elegant, Mei Fong and Andrew Lih, Jeremy Goldkorn, Jorge Guajardo and Paola Sada, Hu Shuli, Elizabeth Knup, Kaiser Kuo, Showkee Lee and Soh and all their kids, Debbie Liang, Guo Liang, Rebecca and Kenny Lin and their children, Angie and Ben, Miranda Ma, Kirk McDonald, Russell Leigh Moses, Evan Osnos, Herve Pauze and Lisa Robins, Fr. Roberto Ribiero, Bipin Rudhee, Diane Sovereign, Peg and Bob Walther, Lily Wang, Bill and Jenny Wright, Anita Zhang, Sellen Zhang.

In China at large: Liam Casey, Brian and Jeanee Linden, Rebecca Mackinnon, Roland Soong, Andy Switky, Sun Zhe and Nina Ni.

My special crew of Chinese language helpers who really stepped up: John Flower and Pam Leonard, who also took us all over Sichuan Province, Sarah Jessup, Chris Livaccari, Orville and Baifang Schell, who have provided endless help in countless ways. My sister, Susan Garau, shares my obsession with language and was always ready to chat about Mandarin. And my many language teachers, from Meng Laoshi to Danny.

Our wonderful friends in the US who encouraged us and sheltered us: Meena and Liaquat Ahamed, Mike Brewer and Janet Brown, Ann Brown, Linc Caplan, Susan DeVogel and Alan Zabel, Patty and Marvin Fabrikant, Julian Fisher, Rebecca Frankel, Katie Hafner, Randy Kluver, Katie Neider, Beth and Charlie Peters,

Lee Rainie, Shaun Raviv, Sherry Smith and Marcus Corley, Sue Tierney, Bill and Lynda Webster.

And the dear friends who dared to visit: Chandler Burr, Gloria Dittus, my cousin Eileen Fischer, Simon Lazarus and Bonnie Rose, Barbara and Robert Liotta, Rita O'Connor and Ted Schell, Ric and Heather Redman and their daughter Jing, Mary Schwab-Stone, Kate Sedgwick, Susan Shirk. Jessica Herzstein and Lyn Jeffery both let me tag along on their amazing work around Shanghai.

Although my husband and I had the idea of moving to China, and I had the idea of immersing myself in Chinese, Rebecca Nicolson and Aurea Carpenter of Short Books were responsible for the idea that I might write about my experience in China by writing about the language. I am very grateful to them for that wonderfully clarifying insight, and for nudging me through all the steps that separate a "book idea" from a finished manuscript. Emily Fox wrangled with all the characters and tone marks, an amazing feat.

Our children, Tom and Lizzy Fallows, and Tad and Annie Fallows, relentlessly emailed, skyped, came to visit, and were very tolerant, patient and loving with their wandering parents. They even seemed happy to have us back home. My mom, Angie Zerad, has been a superstar supporter and enthusiast from start to finish. Jim and I had no idea what we were in for when we set out for China. It was an experience that encompassed everything we naively promised each other many years ago: for better for worse; for richer for poorer; in sickness and in health. China was all of that and much, much more. We had quite a time together. This book is for Jim.